I Couldn't Do This Alone, I Had Help

*I Couldn't Do This Alone,
I Had Help*

Lessons in Management and in Life taught
by EVERY PERSON YOU'LL EVER MEET

MARSHALL KORNBLATT

StoryTerrace

Text Amy Bonnaffons, on behalf of StoryTerrace
Design StoryTerrace
Copyright © Marshall Kornblatt and StoryTerrace
Text is private and confidential

First print April 2023

StoryTerrace

www.StoryTerrace.com

CONTENTS

DEDICATION — 7

1. ORIGINS: FAMILY HISTORY AND EARLY LIFE — 11

2. ADOLESCENCE: GROWING AS A MUSICIAN, BECOMING A YOUNG MAN — 37

3. IN THE ARMY — 47

4. CAREER AND FAMILY LIFE — 63

5. RETIREMENT — 103

DEDICATION

That's me! It's a picture I had done when I retired as President of the Jewish Home of Northeastern PA.

This project began as a way for me to give to my grandchildren, Chava and Shlomo stories and experiences that I had not shared with them. I still hope it performs that function but as the project progressed it evolved into more of a tribute to all of those people who helped me advance as a person and who shaped my life in more ways than I can count. In the final analysis "THAT IS AS IT SHOULD BE".

There were some individuals more directly involved with this effort, whose participation I want to recognize.

I COULDN'T DO THIS ALONE, I HAD HELP

Sheva and me

Sheva Cohen, whose support and consideration allowed me the time and space to work on this document. When you lose a spouse you feel like you'll never have that kind of unconditional acceptance, affection, and support again. You're lucky if you find love once is what you think. Well, my entire book talks about how lucky I've been and my luck didn't run out when I met Sheva Cohen who is the woman I have happily spent the last 5-plus years loving and enjoying. I feel fortunate to have her in my life and I'm grateful for her support, love, and tolerance. In addition, her entire family has welcomed me without reservation and accepted me into their lives as a member of their

I COULDN'T DO THIS ALONE, I HAD HELP

family. This has provided me with the kind of environment that made it easy to relive and document selected portions of my life without the pressure of feeling like I omitted someone or something. So thank you, Jackie, Nate, Eden, Ben, Isaac, Bill, Annie and Kai. It just doesn't get much better than that!

This book is also dedicated to two major influences in my major influences in my life, my father Joseph Kornblatt and my wife, Lillian Kornblatt. Remembering them always brings a smile to my face and every single day the wisdom and the examples they set for me by the way they lived are reflected in my own life.

My sister – Elayne Kornblatt Phillips, Lanie, sometimes my partner in crime, sometimes the injured party in my stunts, but always my advocate and supporter. She's my baby sister and I think she's been better to me than I deserve, but isn't that what sisters are for?

Tom Thompson and me *Susan Herney, Me, Lillian*

I COULDN'T DO THIS ALONE, I HAD HELP

My personal proofreaders, Tom Thompson and Susan Herney both published authors and long-time friends who offered expertise and experience when I had none.

The people at StoryTerrace who made this process so easy and so much fun. Particularly Amy Bonnaffuns and Brian Burnsed, whose talents were so great that you can't see, hear or read their presence because they made their involvement sound just like me.

My final dedication is to anyone who reads this and finds inspiration or meaning or value in the content. My thanks for your willingness to enter my life and consider what I've learned.

With great respect,
Marshall Kornblatt

1
ORIGINS: FAMILY HISTORY AND EARLY LIFE

The story of the Kornblatts in America begins with a tiny ball of dough. My great-grandfather on my father's side, a baker, left Poland with a gooey lump of sourdough starter; he fed and nurtured it on the journey and used it to bake the first loaves for the family bakery he founded in Wilkes-Barre, Pennsylvania. That starter, so carefully transported across the ocean, was the beginning of over 100 years' worth of bread that would feed our family and community for generations. The family bakery stayed open until the 1970s, and a second one, opened by my cousin Ronald Chvotzkin, remained open until the late 1990s.

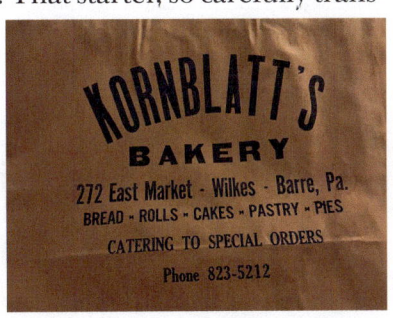

First Kornblatt's bag design
No Area Code
No Zip Code.
Dragnet - JUST THE FACTS
(Old radio fans will get it)

I COULDN'T DO THIS ALONE, I HAD HELP

As for the other side of the family, my great-grandfather Jacob Nudelman came to America with a needle and thread. He was a tailor and had Nudelman's tailor shop in Scranton. "Tailor shop" is an accurate description of Zayde's business ("Zayde" is Yiddish for Grandpa) only

Nudelmans; Sit: Florence - M, Jacob-GGF, Esther-GGM, Sammy-GU; Stand: Libby-GA, Sylvia-GA, Irving-GU, Sol-GF, Becky-GM

if you believe that "boom" is an accurate description of the sound a nuclear bomb makes when detonated. It was really a pawn shop, where people who needed money would bring everything from clothing to shoes, from false teeth to eyeglasses. People wishing to purchase would come in and try on various items and purchase the one with the best fit. Apparently, my great-grandmother—a feisty woman—was well known for handling the drunks.

Both sides of my family came to the United States to escape the persecution that Jews faced in Poland and Russia: Cossacks and pogroms. They chose Wilkes-Barre and Scranton because they knew other Jewish immigrants who had also settled here. On my mother's side, the first to come to the U.S. was her grandfather, who worked and sent money to bring over her father. He thought he had sent enough money for his future son-in-law, Sol Nudelman, to

I COULDN'T DO THIS ALONE, I HAD HELP

come the whole way, but my grandfather got stranded in Amsterdam and had to work as a tailor to pay the rest of his passage to America. Finally, he made it to Scranton, and together, my grandfather and great-grandfather were able to send for their wives and children six or seven years later. During that time, their only communication consisted of letters—infrequent, unreliable, and often redacted due to the intrusive government surveillance of the time. I'm told that when the letters reached my great-grandmother and grandmother, they would have words cut out; they'd always say, "I sent a couple of dollars for you," but there was never any money in the envelope.

My great-grandmother and grandmother came through Ellis Island; my great-grandfather was there to meet them. Fortunately, they passed the health tests and didn't get stranded in immigration limbo or sent back home. My grandmother vividly remembered the day she looked over the side of the boat and saw the Statue of Liberty; she said she thought it was the most beautiful thing she had ever seen. The women on the boat were primarily Jewish, and when the women saw the Statue, they celebrated by throwing their Sheitels—their wigs worn for modesty—into the ocean. My grandmother recalled a sea of wigs bobbing beside the boat. Asked her name at Ellis Island, she said "Rivka"—the Yiddish form of Rebecca; unfamiliar with the name, the immigration officer spelled it "Riwfka."

About 2 years after arriving in Scranton, my great-

I COULDN'T DO THIS ALONE, I HAD HELP

grandmother and grandmother had children a mere handful of hours apart; my great-grandmother gave birth to my mother's uncle, and my grandmother to my mother. When they went to grade school together, she'd call him "Uncle Sammy," much to his annoyance.

When I was born, I had four living grandparents and three living great-grandparents, all of whom lived nearby. My earliest happy memories are of large family dinners. On the Sabbath, or Jewish holidays, there would sometimes be 30 or 40 people –sometimes even more. First, at my maternal great grandmother's house, then at my maternal grandmother's.. She'd have tables set up all over the house—spilling out from the dining room into the hallway and beyond. She was a classic Jewish grandmother, with plastic all over the living room furniture. She used to say, "I'll take the plastic off when you bring the woman you're going to marry!"

There were similar gatherings at my paternal grandparents' house. It was this side of the family that owned the bakery; my father's parents lived in an apartment adjoining it, and my father's brother and his two sisters, along with their husbands and children, all lived above the bakery. We'd call to each other through a window, yelling up and down from the sidewalk. A guy named George owned the bar next door; he'd let us come in and drink birch beer. I remember that George's was one of the first places I ever saw a spittoon.

I COULDN'T DO THIS ALONE, I HAD HELP

Apparently, Grandpa Kornblatt was a very bad gambler. "Bad" both in that he gambled a lot and in that he didn't gamble well. One time, he lost the bakery in a card game. After repurchasing it, my grandmother legally divorced my grandfather and took ownership in the bakery so it would be in her name rather than his. I didn't know about this until recently when a trip to Ancestry.com unearthed the divorce record and a cousin told me the whole story.

I was the first grandchild on my mother's side of the family (and the first male Kornblatt grandchild on my father's). Eventually, there were many cousins, but I got to be the king for a while. I think that's probably where I got my confidence. For a while, at least, I had everyone's attention, and by the time I had to share it, I'd internalized enough self-esteem to last me the rest of my life.

I have few memories of my paternal great-grandmother—who I called "Babu," a version of "Bubbah," Yiddish for grandmother—but I'm told that she adored me. Apparently, when she died, I began talking to an imaginary friend I called "Babu." My mother always wondered whether I was really talking to my great-grandmother's spirit.

My great-grandparents on my mother's side were very observant Jews, and my great-grandfather used to take me to the morning service around seven, before he went to work as a tailor. He was very proud of me—not everybody could bring a great-grandchild with them! I enjoyed it because of the company—it made me feel special to be taken along. But

I COULDN'T DO THIS ALONE, I HAD HELP

what I remember most vividly is the terrible oatmeal they'd serve after the service. It was truly awful: Full of lumps and undercooked, it would crunch when you ate it. I suppose all the old guys at the service were just grateful to have food; most of them were immigrants from Europe and knew what it was to be hungry.

My grandmother's father owned the building they lived in. It had three stories. On the third were my grandparents, on the first were my great-grandparents, and according to rumor, the second floor housed a woman of the night. My great-grandfather made wine in the basement. My grandfather, when he got home, would do a special two-note whistle so that my grandmother, upstairs, would know he had arrived. My grandmother wanted my grandfather to buy a house; she always wanted a home of her own. But my great-grandfather talked my grandfather out of it. "What do you want a house for?" he'd say. "All the taxes, the maintenance . . ." My grandmother never forgave her father for talking her husband out of it. Perhaps he just wanted the rent! Or perhaps he saw their potential homeownership as an unnecessary headache when he could provide housing to them at minimal expense.

My great-grandfather had a blackjack—a piece of lead shaped like a teardrop. He'd put it up his sleeve when he didn't know who was at the door. One time, my great-grandmother said to him, "Jake, you go to the front door, and you have no idea who's there!" He slid the blackjack down into his hand and displayed it to her. "Sure, I don't know who's there," he said. "But I know what I'll do if the wrong person shows up!"

I had an uncle named Irving—Irving Nudelman (my middle name is Irving, after him). He was killed in France, one of the very last casualties of World War II. He'd been studying to be a doctor when he enlisted. Supposedly, he was the kindest, gentlest, most sensitive guy; everyone remembers him fondly. My great grandmother, his mother, got money because he was killed in action; she always called this her "blood money" and would cry every month when it came. Years later, some of the family were visiting the National Museum of American Jewish Military History in Washington, D.C., and they came upon a picture of someone standing and guarding the Tomb of the Unknown Soldier—a very high honor. In immediate recognition, they exclaimed, "It's Isaac!" (his name was Irving in English but Isaac or Yitzchak in Hebrew). The caption below only said, "A Jewish soldier guarding the Tomb of the Unknown Soldier." They went to the head of the museum, eager to identify their relative. The director

Nobody knew my great uncle Irving (Isaac) guarded the tomb of the Unknown Soldier. I'm very proud to have his name.

asked them to produce a few more pictures, to be sure; they did, and now the caption identifies the soldier as Irving Nudelman.

When my mother and father got married, they went to live in apartment in the building owned by my paternal grandmother. My great-grandmother on my paternal side (remember Babu mentioned above) was still alive and also living with my grandparents. When they came in, she immediately started throwing plates at the wall. My mother was shocked at this seeming outbreak of violence—was my great-grandmother trying to throw plates at her? In fact, this was a gesture intending to bring good luck, similar to the crushing of a wineglass under the groom's foot at a Jewish wedding.

No one in my family ever taught Yiddish to me or my sister, though they spoke it fluently; it gave them the perfect way to have private conversations in our presence without worrying about us knowing what was said. They brought some European traditions with them; for example, they made their own gefilte fish. My grandfather had friends who fished in the Lackawanna River, and we'd find carp swimming in the bathtub in my grandmother's home. When it was time, they

That's me around 3 already looking for trouble

would take them out, hit them with a hammer, scale them—I remember scales all over the kitchen—and then grind them up with hand-cranked meat grinders that attached to the side of a table.

My grandmother always said of me, "He's an *active* little boy." Indeed, I got into my share of mischief. I was the first kid in the family to read. Once, when we'd gathered for a big holiday meal—perhaps for Rosh Hashanah or Yom Kippur—I was playing with my cousins, and in a closet, I noticed Feen-a-mint gum—a laxative gum. I knew what it was because, at six or seven, I could read—but none of my cousins could yet. I told them that the gum was Chiclets and passed it out. Soon, the inevitable effects took hold. It was chaos; the grownups were holding the kids over everything that had a hole. Meanwhile, I was standing there like a sea of tranquility in the midst of the storm, perfectly serene. "What did you do?" said my parents. I didn't know how they knew it was me.

I'd be remiss not to mention my aunt Nancy and aunt Pearl—my two favorite aunts. Nancy was my godmother. She got engaged to her husband just so that they could be my godparents. She was so good at it that we made them my son's godparents when he was born. Aunt Nancy never gave me clothing for a birthday gift—always a toy of some sort, which I deeply appreciated. She got me one of my favorite gifts ever, a *Peter Pan* record. Her husband, Paul, was the salt of the earth. Then there were Uncle Jay and Aunt Pearl, my grandfather's sister's daughter and her husband. They had only a few relatives except for us. They weren't really my aunt and uncle, but they were the right age, so that's what they became. Aunt Pearl was my favorite babysitter; she used to tell us stories about Jungle Jim, a fictional, Tarzan-like jungle hero. When I got old enough, I once called her "Pearl" instead of "Aunt Pearl," and she looked so hurt and disappointed that I never did it again—she had no other nieces or nephews, and therefore no one else to call her "aunt." I still remember singing at her wedding, at age five or six.

My dad's father was the first of the grandparents to pass away, when he was in his late 50s. He was a heavy smoker, but I don't know what he actually died of. I remember my dad saying prayers for him and me tagging along. My grandmother, his wife, lived well into her 70s, and my maternal grandparents to around 87 and 96, respectively (we can't be sure of the exact age of anyone from that generation, since so much documentation was lost).

Me, My father (Joseph) my sister Elayne (in stroller). I think that's Atlantic City

My father served in World War Two and earned a Master's degree in social work from Columbia University. He spent

I COULDN'T DO THIS ALONE, I HAD HELP

years helping veterans of the Korean War and World War II find their way through the system of veteran's benefits, particularly the GI Bill. When he got married, he gave this job up and went to work in the family bakery. The bakery actually paid more, but my grandmother never forgave my mother for my father's career change—he was the only child who'd gone to college, and he didn't "use" his degree after his marriage. He used to get up around 4 a.m. and come home around two or three in the afternoon. After taking a nap, he'd be with us for the rest of the day.

My mother worked as a nurse. She took care of us while we were young, and then when I was about 10 years old, she went back to work, taking shifts and doing private duty work. She had wanted to be a doctor and certainly had the ability, but it was difficult for women to enter the medical field beyond becoming a nurse at that time, and her parents didn't support her ambitions. When my mother graduated from nursing school, my maternal grandfather bought a phone for the house so she could get calls to go to work—that was her gift for graduation. This was the very first phone they had in their home, and also the last--an old rotary phone that weighed a ton. My mother was very bitter about the lost opportunity to become a doctor, but she enjoyed and excelled in her work as a nurse; she would refer to many of her younger patients as her "children." My mother's relationship with her parent's was always somewhat distanced as I remember it.

I COULDN'T DO THIS ALONE, I HAD HELP

I remember my parents always being there for us. They must have been absent sometimes, but in my memories, their presence is constant. They really took an interest in their children and nurtured our development. Our home was very rich, culturally and musically. My parents collected all kinds of records, an eclectic smorgasbord of sound; we heard it all. Both of them absolutely adored music. We listened to everything from Robert Louis Stevenson's *Treasure Island*, to Ethel Merman in *Annie Get Your Gun*, to traditional klezmer music and recordings of the world's great cantors. Leonard Bernstein's series *Young People's Concerts* with the New York Philharmonic was required listening.

Artistically, neither of my parents could do anything more than turn on the radio. Neither could play an instrument. My mother thought she could sing because the salesman at the radio store had a band and once told her, "You've got a great voice!" when she sang along to the Victrola. In later years, I used to stop playing when she'd start singing because it was so painful. In any case, it was important to them that we learned the musical skills they lacked. So they started me on the piano when I was four years old.

My first piano teacher was a man from Vienna named Olaf Trygvasson. I remember him as very slender and extremely tall distinguished-looking man with large hands and a very soft voice. He had trained in Europe and performed with orchestras throughout the continent. He fled Europe when Hitler came to power. I studied with him for less than a year

I COULDN'T DO THIS ALONE, I HAD HELP

and performed in my first recital while he was my teacher. (More about that recital in a moment.) When he moved out of town suddenly, I was in need of a new instructor.

Fortunately, my parents looked for the best teacher they could find -- I'm sure partially based on Mr. Trygvasson's opinion of my natural talent. Then I had the great fortune of studying with Anne Liva, a Juilliard-trained pianist who happened to live in Scranton and specialized in teaching young children. Her stellar reputation was 100% deserved. She interviewed every new potential student before accepting them. She listened to you play and gave you an ear test to discover whether you had perfect or relative perfect pitch and spoke with you to ascertain your attention span and ability to understand musical concepts. I remember the interview vividly. After about 15 minutes of examination, she said to my parents "I MUST have this boy!" My life in music began with that statement.

I spent the next 13 years as her student. Not only did Mrs. Liva excel at teaching fundamental skills, but she wove in music theory from the very beginning. She also taught me, by example, how to teach. I'd come back to her techniques when I started giving piano lessons myself. In addition, I learned about inspiring, motivating, critiquing, and setting expectations and goals. These principles and insights would form the basic building blocks of my interactions with people and my management philosophy for the rest of my life.

My first recital, at age four and a half, is the stuff of family

I COULDN'T DO THIS ALONE, I HAD HELP

legend. At that point, I'd been taking lessons for about four or five months; I'd learned perhaps five or six songs. My teacher told my parents that there was a recital coming up, and Mr. Trygvasson told my parents he wanted me to be in it. He thought I was already playing well enough that I should acquire experience performing in public as early as possible. My parents agreed but didn't think much of it. A recital for young beginner students on the second floor of a local music store with a four-or-five-month student playing: how big a deal could it be?

My mother and father showed up at the recital in their work clothes--my dad with flour on his pants from the bakery, my mother in a housedress (thankfully, they had thought to dress me up, since I'd be performing). Immediately upon arriving, they realized they were severely underdressed; the room was filled with people. Men wearing suits and ties, women in furs and dripping with jewelry. Apparently, they hadn't realized just how widely respected Mr. Trygvasson was and the nature of his clients.

My parents sat in the last row, swallowed their embarrassment, and settled in for the recital, hoping no one would see them. I was the very last student to perform. When it was my turn, my teacher stood up to introduce me and said, "Only a handful of times in a teacher's life do they get to work with a young man or woman who has the kind of talent and ability . . ."

Knowing it was my turn, I got up, sat myself at the

piano, and started to play—thereby cutting off the rest of the sentence. I played my songs, did my little bow, and went back to my seat. My teacher continued. "I don't know what else to tell you," he said. "You see what I mean?" Now everyone was looking around to find this child's parents, who were, of course, still trying to be invisible. It turned out that most of the audience were patrons of Kornblatt's Bakery, so they weren't banished from the recital room and the Wilkes-Barre social order. In the spirit of full disclosure, I should say that I don't actually remember that story—I suppose I was too young—but it's been told so many times that I feel like I do.

The confidence I displayed in that anecdote definitely rings true for me, even as a 5-year-old. Even as a child, I never felt any pressure or anxiety about performing in public. I can't explain it nor can I take credit for it, but I've always had confidence in my ability to determine how good I was at something. So if I was comfortable that I was competent I had no reluctance to "show off" and enjoyed being the center of attention, even for a few moments. I would joke that if someone had a flashlight and turned it on I would dance naked in the spotlight and sing two choruses of "Danny Boy" before realizing I wasn't on stage. I have given workshops and performed on piano for audiences of up to 5,000 people when performing behind major headliners.

As a youngster, I played piano, sang, and acted. From piano recitals to school plays, I loved the spotlight; at one point, my parents heard from someone connected to a New York talent agency saying that they would like to represent me and have me audition for Broadway shows. My parents rejected the idea, for which I'm now grateful; the life of a child performer is not an easy one.

From the very beginning, my mother assumed the role of piano practice PITA—a real Pain In The Ass. That is not a slur—it is a compliment. Almost every musician I know needed a PITA when they were initially taking lessons. I am still grateful for her commitment. She accepted no excuses, and I tried plenty. I enjoyed playing, but like many kids, I had other things I wanted to do, and if not for her ruthless insistence, I would have quit piano. As a piano teacher myself, I've seen it countless times: Almost every child will quit unless someone stands next to them every day and makes them do it, saying, "This is good for you—you'll appreciate it someday." My mother took this job very seriously. She never just said, "Go practice. I'll listen from the other room." She'd stand behind me and look over my shoulder. I do remember thinking at the time that if she was willing to stand there while I practiced, it must be important to her, and maybe I should continue. Originally, my mother thought that she could learn to play piano as I learned. That plan was flawed from its inception. In about five weeks, I left her in my dust. As time progressed, I accepted piano practice as part of the habitual rhythm of my day, like brushing my teeth. If a neighbor kid asked me to come outside and

I COULDN'T DO THIS ALONE, I HAD HELP

play baseball before I'd practiced, I'd say, "I'll be there in 30 minutes," and that was that.

My sister played piano too. She didn't have the innate ability I did, but she became a very accomplished pianist. She, being younger, started two years after me, so she usually got pieces I had played a year or more prior. I'd hear her painstakingly work her way through a tune, and then I'd waltz into the room, sit down at the piano, and casually play it twice as fast as she had. Even when she was playing for family or friends, I would follow her performance with my own. Even today, Elayne will say, "I can never play in front of people! It's your fault!" It's true. My bad, my fault—I'm sorry, sis. I adore my sister, but at the time, I was too full of myself.

Elayne and me

I went to regular classes during the day; after school on Monday, Wednesday, and Sunday, we had Hebrew school. The bus came and picked us up at our house and took us to the school building (the building still stands but now houses the Fraternal Order of Eagles). One time, after Hebrew school,

I COULDN'T DO THIS ALONE, I HAD HELP

I went out to the little candy store at the corner—I had a nickel I wanted to spend there—and I missed the bus home. Considering what to do, I remembered that my mother had told me, "If you're ever in trouble, find a policeman." In those days, the policemen used to walk regular beats. I found one and told him what had happened, and he took me in his car and drove me back to the bakery. He even let me play with the siren. My dad called my mother and said, "The police brought your son home." My mother hadn't even known I was missing.

One of my Hebrew school teachers, when I was nine or 10, was named Rabbi Weinstein. One day, I was talking while he was teaching. He asked me to stop; I did, for a few minutes, and then just started up again. This happened a few more times, and then he lost his patience. He took me into the closet, the huge coatroom, and took off his belt. I braced myself, but to my surprise, he just said, "I'm only going to smack the wall, but when you leave here, you better look like I was hitting you." When we came out, the kids were mortified; I can still remember the stricken looks on their faces. But he hadn't touched me—though I'd never tell. THOSE WERE CERTAINLY DIFFERENT TIMES!

I enjoyed playing games in the neighborhood, especially with my friend Melford Ruben, who we called Mouf. After I practiced piano, I'd go over to Mouf's. He had the biggest yard, so we'd go to his place to play stickball. We had a sponge ball, and we'd use a bat or sometimes broomsticks.

I COULDN'T DO THIS ALONE, I HAD HELP

I still remember the route: I'd walk up to the elementary school about 7 doors down from my house, and there was a board knocked out of the fence in the back. If you slid through the opening made by the missing board, you'd find yourself in an alley right across from Mouf's backyard.

My sister and I also played together. I remember many hours of hide and seek. (One time, I hid in the linen closet and my sister in the dryer; that drove my mother crazy.) Frequently, our play sessions ended in tears (usually for her). I'd talk her into doing things she shouldn't have done. One time, I dared her to jump off a roof. I told her I'd done it already and it was fun. Of course, I hadn't actually jumped. It was only about 10 feet off the ground, but when she landed, her knees came up and smacked her face when she hit the ground, and she got a bloody lip. I knew I'd be in trouble with my parents, so I immediately jumped off the roof myself. I wasn't hurt, but now at least they couldn't say I had made her do something I wouldn't do myself. Still, she never let me forget it. She had her moments of revenge, however--but they were rare. On one occasion, she talked me into dressing up in some of her clothes and parading around the house when we had company over. I only did it because of some big secret she would only share after I walked through the house. When I had finished following her on my journey, everyone was laughing except me. Lanie just laughed along with the rest of the family and I realized that the reward wasn't coming and I had been duped. I

I COULDN'T DO THIS ALONE, I HAD HELP

probably smacked her.

Still, despite our occasional antagonism, I loved my sister and wouldn't let anybody hurt her. She is extremely bright and has been all over the world and around the block several times too. This isn't her first rodeo. The reason she is still that gullible (trust me she is) is that my sister is so extraordinarily caring and compassionate and trusting. She just can't conceive of anyone misleading or downright lying to her just for a joke. To be fair, Elayne is wise when someone asks for something of value or a big favor. She is my perfect foil. I adore Elayne, I'm am proud of her accomplishments, and I love being her big brother. To be honest, I'm sorry for the number of times I've taken advantage of her trusting nature - well most of the time anyway - well pretty much most of the time, sort of! I love the fact that my baby sister is my best friend, gives me unconditional support and shares her life with me. She makes me feel valued in a way that only siblings can.

I went to elementary school at Grant Street School. I didn't behave too badly, but I did like to talk, and the punishment in those days was that they'd put you in a coat closet. The closet was the width of the classroom, and each morning, the 20 or 25 kids in the classroom would hang up their coats there. One day, I got put in there for talking, and I came home and told my mother. She was livid. She called the school and let them have it: "Don't you ever do that to a child again!" Indeed, they changed the policy after that.

I COULDN'T DO THIS ALONE, I HAD HELP

I wasn't crazy about school, but plenty of colorful memories stand out in my mind from that time. I remember Miss Murphy, my first-grade teacher who I had a crush on; she was particularly nice. On the other hand, Miss Myers, my fourth-grade teacher, would take a yardstick and smack you behind the legs if you misbehaved. Everyone was scared of Miss Myers. The students called her Cannonball Killer; I have no idea why, but we would laugh when we said it.

Another favorite memory is the time I called the operator and said, "I need to speak with someone in Alaska." I told her that it was for a school project. She was confused, but I talked her into it, and eventually, she complied (I could be very convincing). She connected me with a random number in Alaska that was a general store; I asked what time it was there and how cold it was and I chatted with several employees and some customers. When my mother got the phone bill, she was understandably confused: "Why the hell did we call Alaska?"

I worked in my family's bakery sometimes—mostly putting together cake boxes. I was paid 25 to 50 cents for the day. I remember that bread was 11 cents for a small loaf of rye, 23 cents for a large rye, 40 cents for larger football-shaped rye, and a huge sandwich rye was about 47 cents. On top of that, we gave discounts to clergy--100% off, we never charged clergy or police—so every nun, priest, and rabbi in town patronized our bakery. Later I worked behind the counter dealing with customers filling orders and working the cash register. I was paid hourly wages by that time, but the education I received in customer service and business was priceless.

In winter, in the middle of the school year, the Kornblatts went to Miami. I remember that the first time we took the trip my father called the principal, Mr. Bowen, to let him know and ask if the teachers could provide lesson plans for the next two weeks because my parents insisted that we not fall behind in our studies. That also made it much easier for the school to approve our absence. I remember hearing him say, "Dick, how are ya?" It turned out that he knew the principal from somewhere, but I was just impressed that he was using his first name! My grandparents would actually take the vacation and my mother would go because, as a nurse, she could help look after my grandparents, keep them on their medications, and diagnose any medical issues that came up and take appropriate action. My mother, sister and I were sort of tag-alongs, but we were thrilled to go along, get warm, and return with a tan. We were the envy of every kid in the school.

It was because of these trips that I discovered how much of the school day is basically fluff. My mother would get the outlines of our lessons from our teachers and make sure we did the work, but we were always done in about two hours. When we came back, we always did well on our makeup tests. This made me wonder: What the heck was the point of the other five hours in the school day? I never had to work

I COULDN'T DO THIS ALONE, I HAD HELP

very hard in school, but especially after that, I didn't take it too seriously.

I had a legendary moment with my paternal grandparents during our annual Miami vacation. My mother and sister were invited to dinner and my responsibility was to take grandma and grandpa out for dinner read them the menu and order for them when the waiter came. Neither of them read English although they spoke fluently and this task usually went to my mother. After dinner concluded grandma Kornblatt asked me "Would you like to see a movie?" and my immediate response was "Sure". As we walked I saw a marquis in the distance that said HIDEOUT IN THE SUN which I honestly assumed was a cowboy movie. I said "let's go see that" and we turned and started walking toward the theater. When we got there no pictures were outside the theatre and I realized it was an adult film. My grandparents walked to the ticket booth and asked for "2 adults and 1 child" to which the woman in the booth said "we don't have children's tickets" and so my grandmother said "So we'll pay for an adult" and into the theater we went. As we opened the curtains that separated the lobby from the movie screen to enter I remember a pair of women's breasts on the screen. My grandmother turned around and said, "We're leaving." To which my grandfather spun my grandmother around and said, "We paid – we're staying" and so we did. It was simply about a nudist colony and other than naked people there was nothing more. In fact, it became a cult classic

I COULDN'T DO THIS ALONE, I HAD HELP

movie because the writer and director of the movie was the first woman to be involved in that genre of movies at the director/producer role. I got hell when my grandparents informed my mother about where I'd taken them.

My mother found a way for us to practice piano while we were in Florida. She found a music store with pianos and asked the owner if we could practice there. She offered to pay, but he said no: "Your kids' playing draws customers—bring 'em and let 'em play!" There, I got to play on a piano that the actor and comedian Jimmy Durante had once played. There was a mirrored area above the keys so that they could craft shots in which his hands were visible.

I'll never forget something that happened when I was practicing at the piano store. I was happily playing, pleased with myself as usual, when a gentleman came up and watched me play. He asked if I would play "Gitanerias" again—a classical concert piece by Cuban composer Ernesto Lecuona, who also wrote "Malaguena." I had played it earlier and I thought he must have been so impressed he wanted to hear it again. Pleased to show off, I quickly ripped through the tune nonchalantly: faster than the piece should have been played, but well enough for this gentleman to be pleased that I'd fulfilled his request (or so I thought). Then he said, "May I?" and sat down at the piano. "I want to show you something," he said. He played the song himself—*really* well, much better than I had done. After finishing, he turned to me and said, "Don't ever assume your audience doesn't

I COULDN'T DO THIS ALONE, I HAD HELP

know more about the music than you do. Play as though everyone listening is an expert." It turned out that he was a concert pianist coming to the piano store to decide which Steinway he wanted to play for an upcoming concert. That was an excellent lesson for me as a performer, one I never forgot. It was a lesson that turned out to apply to more than just piano playing; when I got older and got into business, I thought of it often. Regardless of someone's position in the company, I always assumed they knew as much as I did and treated them as well as I treated my own boss.

2

ADOLESCENCE: GROWING AS A MUSICIAN, BECOMING A YOUNG MAN

A turning point in my childhood came when my father passed away. I was 15 years old. When I think about my dad now, I feel sad that he didn't live long enough for us to become peers—to be adults together, to share experiences and jokes as fellow men. But I am grateful for the years I had with him. He was a wonderful man—kind, gentle, and generous. He did so much for the community and was beloved by a huge number of people. He was very involved in bowling, an active member of two different leagues. One of my favorite memories involves watching him sit at the kitchen table, writing on 3x5 cards, doing calculations related to bowling—figuring out averages, tallying members' dues. At the time, it seemed very technical and impressive. My sister says that what she remembers most about him were his hugs.

They had to open two additional areas of the funeral

I COULDN'T DO THIS ALONE, I HAD HELP

parlor to accommodate the size of the crowd that came to pay their respects. I learned that it was possible to live your life in a manner that would make others not only respect you but feel so favorably toward you that they would make the effort to be in your presence one last time.

After my dad died, we became isolated from the bakery. I remember one day when my mom sent me to the bakery to get milk; we used to just walk into the bakery and take things, casually, without paying. But this time, my grandmother saw me take the milk and said, "Where are you going with that? You have to pay." Just like that, the special relationship with the bakery was over.

Early 70"s playing Jazz with other young musicians. I forgot about the sideburns!

I COULDN'T DO THIS ALONE, I HAD HELP

Meanwhile, I was growing up. Mostly, I was growing as a musician. Before I hit high school, I had already started landing paying gigs around town. This happened organically; my parents' friends and people in the community had seen me play in talent shows or at the Jewish Community Center, and they'd pay me 15 or 20 dollars to perform at their parties. Soon, I was playing so much that the local musicians union started to take notice. When I was 13, the head of the union came to my mother and told her I was playing too many jobs. I had to join, he said, or they'd blackball me. So of course I joined!

I'll never forget the night I met Spencer Cottman. I had recently joined the union, and as a union member, I had been invited to the annual banquet. My mother dropped me off, and I was pretty pleased with myself—dining and watching all of the biggest and best musicians in town. In one jam session, I saw Spencer play for the first time. An extremely talented Black saxophone player, he played like Charlie Parker and sang like Nat King Cole. He was *the* jazz player in the area—the best we had. I was inspired by his playing, and—with my typical confidence—decided that I'd get up and join a jam session. I played "Somewhere Over the Rainbow" with a few of the best musicians (Spencer, Pete DeMarzo, Joe Fox, and Gino Marchetti). I really showed off—displaying my chops, I went up and down the keyboard, playing more notes than that song ever had in its entire life. While I played, Spencer started heading toward

I COULDN'T DO THIS ALONE, I HAD HELP

me; he stood close while I finished the song. I'd noticed him there and was eagerly anticipating his feedback, which I was sure would be positive. But when I'd finished playing, he only remarked, "Kid, you're never gonna know how to play until you learn which notes to leave out." I was immediately put in my place and taught a great lesson.

Soon after that, Spencer called and asked my mother if he could take me around on some of his gigs: "Your son is very talented—I'd like to take him around and let him learn while we play." My mother agreed, largely because Spencer promised to keep me out of trouble. And so, as a young teenager, I started traveling the nightclub circuit with the best jazz musicians in town. My role during these gigs was very specific. At the time, Spencer played with a keyboard player named Jesse Wayde. He was a great pianist and I learned a lot by watching him play and discussing music with Spencer and Jesse. Unfortunately, Jesse was an alcoholic and at the time had little control over his drinking. My job was to wait until the point in the night when Jesse started to pass out, and then I would take

Jesse Wade (left), Spencer Cottman (right). In addition to Mrs. Liva they were my music mentors.

I COULDN'T DO THIS ALONE, I HAD HELP

his place and finish out the night. Jesse eventually gave up drinking, thankfully. But it was during those nights that I really developed skills as a performer. To this day, I credit Spencer with giving me many of the lessons that ensured my later success—not to mention the amazing experience of honing my chops with top-notch musicians and benefiting from his mentorship. Perhaps this goes without saying, but he was ABSOLUTELY VICIOUS about keeping the promise he'd made to my mother. He watched me like a hawk and made sure I never got into any trouble. "I told your mother!" he'd always say.

Meanwhile, of course, I was in high school, where I learned the trumpet in order to play in the marching band (you couldn't walk with a piano). Our teacher, Mr. Ayers, was a very good band instructor, and we had the last all-boy marching band in the city; all the others had gone co-ed, but at GAR high school girls could be majorettes, cheerleaders, or flag-holders and that was all. We'd play a different show each week with different formations. He demanded that we read our music.

My parents, when they went to visit on parents' night, would always save Mr. Ayers for last, alongside the biology teacher, Mr. Chesney, my biology teacher with whom I got along well. Though I always got Bs and As, the teachers knew I wasn't working at my full potential and never hesitated to tell my parents how I could be doing better—but Mr. Chesney and Mr. Ayers had nothing but praise for me, so

I COULDN'T DO THIS ALONE, I HAD HELP

my parents went home with smiles on their faces.

Mr. Ayers had a student teacher while we were there, a man by the name of Agesino Primatic. One day, he said something that ticked me off—I can't remember what. At any rate, I just stared at him for the next half hour. I didn't say anything, just burned a hole through him with my eyes. Finally, he sent me to the principal's office. I remember the principal's confusion: "What exactly did you do?" "I stared," I said honestly. "That's all?" the principal retorted. He called Mr. Primatic: "What did he do?" *pause* "That's all?" *pause* "Please come and see me after your class." *pause* "And YOU go back to class!" In any case, Agesino and I became good friends later on, and neither of us can remember what set the incident off. He moved away and has since passed away but we laughed over the incident many times.

Another musical mentor who came into my life around this time was a man by the name of Patrick Marcinko. He had two sons, Pat and Marko, as well as two daughters, Margret and Charlene. He was a high school music instructor and played trombone and percussion in big bands. The Marcinkos were an incredibly musical family. The elder Pat led a Russian Orthodox choir that toured all over the world. Pat composed liturgical music that is performed by choral groups everywhere. Marko is now the Director of Jazz Studies at Pennsylvania State University School of Music, Artistic Director of the Scranton Jazz Festival and was the drummer with Maynard Ferguson's Big Bop Nouveau

I COULDN'T DO THIS ALONE, I HAD HELP

band. Young Pat teaches high school music, plays regularly with local bands, and took over his father's role with the Russian Choir, carrying on his dad's legacy. One of the daughters sings opera professionally and both daughters play instruments. We would often joke that you had to audition to become part of that family. Pat the elder was one of the greatest educators I have ever known and one of the nicest people and most generous musicians that ever played music. I played with one or more of the Marcinkos in big bands, small groups, and in a group called the Upper Valley Winds—a kind of supergroup from the lower New York and Upper Pennsylvania regions, the best musicians we could find. I played with them under Mr. Marcinko first and then under Pat's direction after his father's death.

I met Pat, the elder, when I was about 14 or 15, and he gave me the chance to play in one of his bands. He was absolutely an educator at heart and taught me everything I needed to know about how to behave—how to show up on time, when to take breaks, how to get the guys back to the music stand. If Spencer was my chief musical influence during this time, Pat taught me what I needed to know about the business side of things and how to be a professional.

My area of Northeastern Pennsylvania had many great musicians, in part because it was an immigrant city; a lot of the kids there came from European families, where music was held in high regard. Tommy Dorsey and Jimmy Dorsey were born here, as well as Ray Anthony, Fred Waring, and

I COULDN'T DO THIS ALONE, I HAD HELP

a whole host of other musicians who've gone on to play venues like Radio City Music Hall. The audiences here were notoriously tough; they brought fruit with them to the shows, and it wasn't to eat. There was an old vaudeville saying: "If you think you're good, try Wilkes-Barre."

When I was about 15, I put together a trio of my own, with a guitar player, Jeff Slavin, and a drummer, Donald Bick. I played on a Silvertone organ made by Sears. We learned that the local Holiday Inn was looking for a band, and we decided to go for it. When we approached the guy who managed the place, his first response was, "How old are you?! I don't need a teenage band." We entreated him to at least listen to us and give us a chance. He agreed, and we played our set—I remember playing "Shangri-La" and "The Lady Is a Tramp." We were much better than he'd expected; he was impressed. He spoke to us afterwards: "You must be 18 to work here. NOW ARE YOU 18?" We all smiled and nodded. Whether or not he believed us, he was ready to book us for 15 dollars apiece for 3 hours—but in the end, we couldn't take the gig because none of us could drive, and none of our parents were willing to shuttle us to and from late-night performances. But we did start playing around town—mostly private parties and bar mitzvahs. It was a pleasure to play with Jeff and Donald, both of whom were excellent musicians. We helped each other grow as musicians and collaborators. Donald would go on to become one of the top timpanists in the country, if not the world,

I COULDN'T DO THIS ALONE, I HAD HELP

playing with the National Symphony and recording for Deutsche Grammophon.

When I was about 16, I started playing for David Blight, who had a dance studio in town and hosted a local TV show. David was a great dancer and narrowly missed a chance to become a regular dancer on *The Lawrence Welk Show* (I once got the chance to see his audition tape!). I remember that when I was little, my sister and I once spotted him at a restaurant; he was a big star to us, and we went up to him and got his autograph. Years later, he somehow got my name; he called and asked if I wanted to be one of his studio musicians.

David had a piano player by the name of Val Gavlick, who really taught me how to accompany people (an entirely different skill from playing on your own). The other exciting thing about working at the dance studio was that suddenly—remember, I was 16—I got to be among so many girls there. I ended up dating several of them. One of the girls at the studio ended up becoming a Rockette and entering the Miss USA pageant; her talent was tap dance, and I played for her in her audition as her accompanist.

Meanwhile, we'd go to the Catskills every summer. In addition to learning the facts of life from the New York kids—who were much more advanced than we were—my sister and I had a great time participating in dance, music, and other activities. It really was like *Dirty Dancing*.

3

IN THE ARMY

After graduating from high school, I enrolled in Wilkes College. I entered as pre-med—much to my mother's delight—but had trouble focusing on my classes and ended up failing everything but health (I ended the semester with an embarrassing .75 cumulative average).

Recognizing that I clearly wasn't ready for college, I decided to pivot and join the military. This was in the middle of the Vietnam War. At that time if you enlisted before you were drafted, you could still choose your specialty rather than being sent right into the infantry. I had an instinct—which luckily turned out to be correct—that the military would be a good place for me to

Entering the Army January 1966. I had no idea what the future had in store for me.

47

gain some discipline, see the world, and learn how to be an adult.

When I took the initial battery of tests at the recruitment office, I was told, "You can do pretty much anything—you have some of the best scores we've seen at this facility." When I asked, "What does that mean?" the recruiter responded with a list of options: "You can do X, or Y and showed me a page of Military Occupational Specialties (MOS). . . or you can do this other thing, but it will require a commitment of four years rather than three, and we can't tell you what it is, and you won't be able to talk about it." Without hesitating, I said, "I want to do that one."

Why did I choose the mystery option, without knowing a single thing about what I'd be asked to do? Well, the easiest answer is that I was young and stupid. But I think there was something intriguing to me (and flattering to my GPA-bruised ego) about doing something different and special, something that required an extra level of trust and discernment. I got to tell people, when they asked what I was doing, "If I told you, I'd have to kill you."

Incidentally, on that topic, there is much about my wartime experience that I still can't discuss because I have no idea whether portions of it are still classified. I had a top-secret cryptographic access authorized clearance, which was the highest security clearance issued at the time. I was thoroughly vetted for this—they contacted many people I knew, all the way down to my optometrist, to get information

I COULDN'T DO THIS ALONE, I HAD HELP

about me. During my service, if they had documents that needed to be transported someplace, they would handcuff a briefcase to my wrist. Sometimes, in these cases, I would boot a colonel or general out of his seat because I needed to get the documents someplace urgently. Though some information has since been declassified, there's much that I still don't feel comfortable sharing. But I did learn many lessons during my time in the military that would apply in all areas of my subsequent life.

At the time, I couldn't have known just how well the "mystery job" would suit me—all I knew was that I had passed some kind of test and signed up for an intriguing new chapter in my life.

When I went home and told my mother I'd enlisted, she went ballistic: "You did *what*?!" She immediately called the nearby Kingston recruitment office, and when she was told, "We've never heard of Marshall Kornblatt," she assumed the whole thing had been a prank. "What the hell did you do that for?" she asked me. "You put me through all that worry for nothing!" I told her I'd been serious and she should: "Call the Wilkes-Barre office!" She did, and when she announced herself as "Mrs. Kornblatt," the voice on the other end immediately said, "Congratulations, Ma'am." She slammed the phone down in defeat.

I did my basic training at Fort Dix, New Jersey. The training was mostly physical, but it was also there that I started to realize how important it would be to build

I COULDN'T DO THIS ALONE, I HAD HELP

relationships with my colleagues and superiors. I did very well there and was promoted to E2 (everyone started as an E1) before I left.

Before leaving Fort Dix, I was given another battery of tests, including one to see if I could read Morse code (an alphabet composed of dots and dashes used in communications environments). I did quite well; it was all just rhythm, so as a musician, it came naturally to me. They played the dots and dashes, shorter and longer tones, and asked me to write them down; I was there after everybody else had left. My success on the assessment gave me the opportunity to become what we called a "diddy-bop"—a person who monitored Morse code transmissions as part of the eavesdropping process. I turned down the opportunity, thinking it didn't sound like much fun. In retrospect, I think this was the right decision—being a diddy-bop was tedious work indeed, and my "mystery" assignment turned out to suit me quite well.

From there, I went to Fort Devens in Massachusetts for advanced specialty training. There, I met the unforgettable Colonel Lewis Lee Millett. He was the commanding officer of ASA, the Army Security Agency, which was my branch of the service. Millett looked almost like a caricature of a general: big barrel chest, handlebar mustache. He had the Congressional Medal of Honor and every award for valor that the United States offered, but he did not have the good conduct medal because he had never gone four straight years without charges. Needless to say, he was quite tough and very much his own person. In fact, he had gone AWOL (absent without leave) when the United States didn't enter World War II fast enough for his liking. When we did finally enter the war, he came back, and instead of court-martialing him when he returned, they just reenlisted him. The rumor at the time was that he was a national hero in France and DeGaulle had issued him the French Legion of Honor--so a court-martial would be seen as an insult to the French. It sounded like it could be true but further investigation showed what actually happened. In 1941 President Franklin D Roosevelt said no Americans would fight on foreign soil. Millett did go AWOL and joined the CANADIAN Army. He was in England in 1942 when the United States entered the war. He applied for and received a transfer back to the US Army. It took the Army about a year to realize that Millett had in fact gone AWOL from the US Army and he was about to be charged with DESERTION. However, during that time he had been serving combat in North Africa where he had earned a Silver Star for bravery by driving a burning halftrack loaded with ammunition away from US troops and jumping out just before it exploded. If that wasn't enough he was famous for was leading the U.S. Army's very last bayonet charge.

At Fort Devens, I think I had my first personal encounter with antisemitism. When we entered the mess hall, we were supposed to take off our hats. If someone ever forgot, they were usually asked, "Are you Jewish? No? Then get your

I COULDN'T DO THIS ALONE, I HAD HELP

[expletive] hat off!" This happened to me one day when I'd forgotten to remove my hat. But of course, when the sergeant asked me, "Are you Jewish?" I responded, "Yes, Sergeant." From that day on, I consistently drew KP duty—the worst and dirtiest job, scrubbing and cleaning the grease trap. In the six or eight months I'd been in the service up until that point, I'd gotten a typical rotation of assignments and hadn't pulled KP much. But after that day, my name showed up on kitchen duty more than anyone else's. I could only conclude that the shift had resulted from the revelation of my Jewish identity. But there was nothing I could do to protest—he was a sergeant, and I just a private.

However, there's a light at the end of this story. At Fort Devens, they had pianos in the officers' clubs, and I used to play in my spare time. One day, Colonel Millett walked in—he of the handlebar mustache and infamous bayonet charge—and noticed me playing.

"Hey," he said, "will you play 'Malaguena' for me?" (Incidentally, this was a piece by Ernesto Lecuona, who'd composed the piece I butchered as a youngster in the Miami piano store).

"Sure," I said. Having learned my lesson in Miami, I played it as well as I possibly could.

When I finished, he asked if I'd play a USO show for him the next day. They had somebody coming into the base he wanted to impress. Of course I agreed and played the show. Afterward, he shook my hand and said, "You'll never pull

I COULDN'T DO THIS ALONE, I HAD HELP

another day of KP as long as you're here." He couldn't have had any way of knowing how frequently I'd been stuck with KP duty; he was just offering to do me a favor in return for helping him.

Of course, the anti-Semitic sergeant didn't know this. The next day, when I went into the mess hall and pulled KP duty yet again, I told him what the colonel had said, but he didn't believe me: "Get in the grease trap!" he yelled. I tried to protest, but he wasn't having it. Finally, I acquiesced and got started cleaning. Two hours later, the doors flew open, and Colonel Millett busted in. He looked around the room and bellowed, "Where's my pie-anuh player?!" I raised my hand. He turned to the sergeant.

"Didn't he tell you that I told him he'd never pull another day's KP?"

"I told him," I hollered, up to my knees in grease.

The Sergeant swallowed hard and I climbed out of the grease trap.

That Sergeant wasn't there the next morning. I don't know where they sent him, but I never saw him again.

My first duty after that was in Synop, Turkey, a little peninsula that jutted out into the Black Sea, right across from the Kamchatka Peninsula (where Russia had its Cosmodrome—the main reason we were there). This was an isolated duty station, which meant that there was no on-base housing; few of the men were married, and no one had their family there.

I COULDN'T DO THIS ALONE, I HAD HELP

The journey to the base was memorable: you'd fly into Istanbul and then board a Black Sea steamer that would take you to Synop. It was about a two-day trip aboard the steamer, and what I mostly remember was how seasick everyone got. For some reason, I was immune; I remember eating the other guys' rejected dinners.

While I was there, there was a sergeant in charge of the operation; his name was Roy Graves. He was about to retire and had started retiring on the job—really taking it easy. He was a nice man, and we got along well. Knowing my performance background, he asked me to take responsibility for giving tours to congressmen and senators. I was happy to do it; the guests appreciated my friendliness and stage presence, and he got a lot of credit. This gave me high visibility on the base, which worked to my advantage. I'd left Fort Devins as an E-3 (Private First Class); while I was there, he promoted me to E-4 (Corporal) and as I departed I was promoted to E-5 (Sergeant).

During my time in Turkey, I got to tour Istanbul; I saw the Blue Mosque and a lot of other gorgeous architecture from the Byzantine empire. I met some Turkish people in Synop and even got to play music in some of the hotels downtown. I remember one day going to see an American movie in town. It was in English, with Turkish subtitles, so I thought I'd have no problem understanding. However, what I failed to realize was that the locals would talk all through the movie (I suppose they thought there was little point in

I COULDN'T DO THIS ALONE, I HAD HELP

listening, since they could read the subtitles). I couldn't hear a thing!

Another fun memory from Turkey came about when a USO show came to our base. The act was Sid and Yvonne, a gentleman and his wife who danced—but they had no music! So they asked if anyone on the base played piano, and I ended up playing for them. I remember that they autographed a picture for me and thanked me for working with them.

During this time, I had several early lessons in leadership. One came about when a few of the guys who worked with me called late at night—clearly drunk—and told me they'd been arrested in downtown Synop. They were laughing, as though we were in the realm of hilarious drunken hijinks, but in fact, this was a terrifying call to receive; if you were arrested in Turkey, you could be put through the Turkish judicial system—with who knows what harsh consequences—and there was very little the United States could do about it. I quickly set about trying to do damage control. I called the base commander and told him what had happened; we needed to try and intercede before they went to trial. But while we were still figuring out our strategy, the guys called me back and confessed that the whole thing had been a joke. "Well, you better go get arrested then," I said, "because the world is about to come down on that jail!" I called back the base commander and told him what had happened. "I'm gonna kill those guys!" he fumed. But I talked him down:

"Please let me handle it," I said. "I promise, I won't let them off easy." He agreed; he trusted me.

When the guys got back, I made sure that they understood how serious their infraction had been and told them they weren't allowed to go downtown for a month. This was an unpleasant punishment—to be stuck on the little base in Synop—but they knew they'd gotten off easy. They could have been sent to the base commander, reassigned somewhere else, or even thrown out of ASA. So they were forever grateful, knowing that I'd spared them a worse fate. In return, they worked their butts off, doing anything I asked.

The military has a lot of rigid rules, with specific consequences. But in this case, I felt it was important that the punishment fit the crime. They were drunk and made bad decisions; who hasn't? In fact, I myself had had to be carried home one night from downtown Synop, early in my time there, so I was hardly qualified to cast the first stone at their behavior. I learned from that instance that it was possible to hold people accountable for mistakes without sacrificing empathy and flexibility.

This is the two seater F4-D Phantom. If you look closely you can see the back seat.

This was my flight console. I had primarily electronic equipment while the pilot had flight controls and gauges.

A patch says it all.
WE WEREN'T THERE
WE WERE NEVER THERE
WE DON'T EXIST
VIGILENT ALWAYS
Eagle grips lightning
ASA LOGO

My 2023 reunion in Japan with Joe Peters, a friend from the service I had not seen since 1969.

I COULDN'T DO THIS ALONE, I HAD HELP

After Synop, I went back to NSA and worked in Fort Meade, Maryland, before getting assigned overseas. My assignment included flying, which I was excited about. My favorite comic books as a kid were the Superman ones (because he flew), and my favorite story was *Peter Pan*; I'd sometimes dreamed of getting my pilot's license. My job wasn't flying planes, but I got to sit in the backseat of a F4D Phantom fighter aircraft (my strong stomach, proven on the Black Sea steamer, helped a lot in this position!). I was what they call a RIO—a Radio Intercept Operator. Among other duties my job was to make sure that radar didn't lock onto the plane so that a SAM (Surface to Air Missile) wouldn't blow us out of the air. I'd tell them to take action if needed. I had the ability to drop chaff, which consisted of tiny pieces of metal that would mask the outline of the plane, or flares. What I learned from doing this job was how to compartmentalize my life. You couldn't pay attention to anything else when you were doing that job; you had to be laser-focused.

We'd fly these missions in Vietnam after departing from a number of locations, often outside Vietnam. When we were in country, we used Tan Son Nhut airbase near Saigon. When I wasn't flying a mission, I was based in Japan. I was on Hokkaido, the northernmost island—that's where Sapporo is, where the 1972 winter Olympics were held. At this point, I was an E-6—a staff sergeant—and I got to pick my own crew, a "trick," which is what they called a shift. I picked guys who were like me: they'd joined because they were in

I COULDN'T DO THIS ALONE, I HAD HELP

danger of getting drafted or because they wanted to pick their own specialty instead of being a grunt in the infantry.

I made a point of treating everyone exactly as I would want to be treated. I told the guys, "We aren't gonna overdo the military stuff, but we are going to do the best work on this base." And we did. Every time there was an important mission, we got picked. (The relationships we built there were so solid that many of those guys are still my friends today. One of them, Terry Brown, founded a successful company after leaving the military and bought a huge farm; every year, up until COVID-19, he held a reunion for us where we'd eat, drink beer, reminisce, and ride motorcycles.)

One of the most exciting moments in that period came when we had the chance to work Apollo 13. They dedicated all of the United States' electronic resources toward the mission—measuring telemetry from the capsule, monitoring the astronauts' respiration and blood pressure, so we at the base became part of that effort. We were never out of touch; there were never any dark times, except when they went around the back side of the moon. It was neat to be part of that mission, even in our own small way.

Another moment that stands out in my memory was seeing images of downtown Wilkes-Barre on TV in Japan. This was just after the Chappaquiddick incident, in which Ted Kennedy's negligent driving had led to the death of Mary Jo Kopechne, who happened to be from Wilkes-Barre. They held the trial in the Wilkes-Barre courthouse, so

I COULDN'T DO THIS ALONE, I HAD HELP

images of my hometown were broadcast across the world. I remember telling all my friends, "That's right where I live!"

Japan was incredible. I was lucky enough to get to experience some of the local culture and even to participate in the music scene there. I started playing in the nightclub district, called Siskino. One night, when I was playing downtown, a guy came up to me and asked if I'd like to work with the band on the Japanese version of *The Tonight Show*, on NHK. So I played for about a month with that band; I was the only American. It was a great deal of fun. This was yet another example of how my music has allowed me to go places, and interact with people, that I would never have had the chance to otherwise. Everywhere you go, there are people interested in music.

While I was in Japan, I wrote letters to my great-grandmother—*only* to her. I knew she didn't hear as much from the family as she'd have liked; usually people would only reach out on her birthday or other special occasions. But when I started writing to her from Japan, everyone else in the family would be forced to call her to find out how I was doing. She couldn't read English, so her son or daughter-in-law would read the letters to her, but she remembered everything and took pleasure in reporting on my welfare and activities when people called. I got a lot of fulfillment from writing those letters to her because I knew that they had an impact on her life.

I learned a lot of important lessons in the service. It was

I COULDN'T DO THIS ALONE, I HAD HELP

the first time in my life that I was thrust into an environment with lots of different people, from different backgrounds, all of whom I had to get along with. I learned how to make friends with everyone, just by paying attention to them. All you have to do, I discovered, is ask someone about themselves, shut up, and listen. People love to feel heard and seen—and I genuinely enjoyed hearing their stories. Truly, everyone you meet has something to offer, something to teach you; this would become a cornerstone of my life philosophy, but the military was the place I learned it first. As a result, I made many friends there and had very few enemies.

That was my first chance to be an authorized leader, too, and to hone some of my natural gifts into usable skills. I found, when I returned, that the skills I'd picked up translated seamlessly into my musical career. The leadership skills I developed in the army were identical to the skills required for leading a band.

I also learned patience; in the military, there are sometimes emergencies or things that need immediate attention, but there's also a lot of waiting. I learned how to make the best out of a bad situation because there were plenty of them. Finally, I learned the importance of honesty. Since then, I have believed it is important to never lie. A lie of omission is as bad as a lie of commission. I would always tell people, "I won't lie. I'll tell you the truth, and I'll be as candid as I can, and if I can't share something, I will say I cannot share that

I COULDN'T DO THIS ALONE, I HAD HELP

with you. And that's gonna be it. If you want me to just tell you what you wanna hear, I'll be glad to do that, but don't hold me accountable later." This served me well in building trust with my colleagues and those who worked for me.

4

CAREER AND FAMILY LIFE

Back to School

When I got out of the military, I went back home and re-enrolled at Wilkes, despite my poor first-semester record there; this time, I was ready. I'd gained maturity and focus during my years in the army, and I also had a more realistic sense of my skills and interests. I scrapped the idea of becoming a doctor and majored in business instead.

I majored in marketing and sales, thinking that this would give me practical skills that would translate into a well-paying job after graduation. This time, I excelled in my classes across the board--but never more so than in the music class I took my first semester. I showed up for the first day of class without telling the instructor anything about my background. On one of the first days, he lectured about how music could create imagery; he played us several selections

I COULDN'T DO THIS ALONE, I HAD HELP

from Aaron Copland's *Rodeo* and asked us what images the music made us see in our mind's eye. Knowing the piece well, I decided to have a little fun with the assignment. When the "Hoedown" movement came on, he asked what we saw, and I said, "People dancing." He lit up: "That's exactly right!" In the next selection, "Moonrise on the Prairie," I said, "I see the stars and a dark moonlit night . . ." Again, he exclaimed at the seeming accuracy of my imagination. However, at one point he looked a me sternly and I stopped immediately. At the end of the lesson, when he asked if anybody had prior knowledge of this piece of music, I fessed up. After the class, I said, "I hope I wasn't being too rude—I studied with Anne Liva for a number of years and I'm familiar with this particular piece." He was nice about it, and after that, he'd always give me the conductor's score to follow along when the class listened to music.

Throughout my college years, I continued playing music professionally. I put together my first jazz band, which played locally. I frequently saw my childhood friend Jody Bush with the New York Times Band, which featured Spencer Cottman's son Spike as their vocalist. I also continued playing for David Blight's school of dance and picked up gigs in the Poconos.

I COULDN'T DO THIS ALONE, I HAD HELP

Love and Marriage

This doesn't belong here but it's my favorite picture of my son Joseph with Lillian's Grandmother Labeba. I adored her.

Lillian and me December 1974. The mustache and long hair went well with bell bottoms and platform shoes.

Also during this time, one of the most consequential events of my life came to pass: I met Lillian, the woman who would become my wife.

That night, I was playing with a trio in the cocktail lounge of a place called the Hotel Casey. Lillian, at the time, was working there as the banquet coordinator. She had a background in design—a degree from the Pratt Institute in New York and experience working as a wallpaper designer—but had returned to Scranton to help out when her father got sick, and accepted a job at the hotel designing centerpieces and things like that.

In a break between sets, I noticed Lillian; she was at the bar, and a drunk customer seemed to be annoying her. Hoping to help ease the situation, I came up to her, put my

I COULDN'T DO THIS ALONE, I HAD HELP

arm around her, and said, "Hey, honey, how are you?" The drunk guy looked from me to her and said, "This is your boyfriend?" She nodded, and he backed off. I apologized for my intrusion: "I hope you don't mind—you seemed miserable." "That's all right," she said. "I was."

We talked for a while, and at the end of the night, I invited her to go with us to another bar called the Red Lion—a jazz bar, the kind where the owner has a gun below the counter but the music is great. She accepted; we stayed out till about 1 a.m. We had such a nice time that I wanted to get in touch with her the next day, but I realized that I hadn't gotten her phone number or her address. I didn't even know her last name. All I had to go on were a few scraps of fact.

One was that she worked at a department store in Scranton called Oppenheim's Dry Goods. I called the store and asked the receptionist, "Is there anyone who works there by the name of Lillian?" The receptionist laughed. "We've got about 70 of them," she said. The place was huge—at least six stories, probably over a five hundred employees.

Undeterred, I decided to pursue my next lead: Lillian had mentioned that she had an uncle who owned a drugstore. So I called every drugstore in Scranton, asked to speak to the owner, and inquired if they had a niece named Lillian. They all said no, until I did reach her uncle. When I explained why I was calling, he just snapped, "If she wanted you to have her number, she'd have given it to you!" and slammed down the receiver.

I COULDN'T DO THIS ALONE, I HAD HELP

Finally, I remembered that Lillian and I knew someone in common, a vocalist named Paulette Costa. I called Paulette and asked for Lillian's number, and the rest, as they say, is history.

We started dating exclusively about a month after our first date. I remember once, early on, telling her that I "needed space" because I didn't want to get too involved. But within a week, I'd called her back and said, "This isn't working for me." I knew I had met someone special.

I remember going to her parents' home for Christmas when we'd been dating for about four or five months. Her parents' home had a commercial garage attached to the building; it had a high ceiling, and I climbed a ladder to retrieve some canned goods off a high shelf for her mother. Suddenly, I felt a tremor at the bottom of the ladder; I looked down to see that Lillian's father was gripping the base of it. He shook it gently and then asked, ominously, "When are you and my daughter going to get married?" "Pretty soon," I replied weakly. What else could I say?

But the truth was that she and I had already talked about marriage; we knew we were serious. I proposed to Lillian about nine months into our relationship, with an engagement ring stuffed in about 100 layers of tissue paper in a giant box I had delivered to the house (we were already living together at that point).

"What's this? It's very light," she said as she picked up the box.

I COULDN'T DO THIS ALONE, I HAD HELP

"I don't know," I said. "Let's see."

I hadn't put my name on it, nor a return address. She opened it up, peeling back all the layers of packaging. When she finally uncovered the box, she knew exactly what it was. "Does this mean we're getting married?" she asked, looking up at me. "I hope so!" I said.

Lillian was Lebanese, and her family had both Melkite and Maronite members. Those are the two major religious sects in Lebanon. She told me soon after our engagement that she planned to convert to Judaism: "It's no good to have two religions in a household." She decided that if she was going to convert, she would do it the most rigorous way possible so that nobody could ever accuse her kids of not being Jewish. She went ultra Orthodox. I had a friend who was an Orthodox rabbi; Rabbi Katz was the principal of the local Hebrew school, and I'd played piano without compensation for their events and graduations. I told him that my fiancée wanted to convert, and he put me in touch with Rabbi Michael Fine who agreed to work with Lillian mostly because Rabbi Katz had asked him. I don't think he had done conversions often, if ever. Now, Jews are supposed to make conversion difficult; he told Lillian, before starting to work with her, "This is going to be very difficult." Separately, he told me, "We're going to do this for two years, and there's a possibility that at the end of it, I may decide she's not ready, and that I don't see it in her future." My response to that was, "Well, at the end of two years,

I COULDN'T DO THIS ALONE, I HAD HELP

I may decide to marry her anyway." But as it happened, his concern was misplaced; Lillian excelled in her studies, and the rabbi adored her. They became very close, and he always spoke warmly of her. He always said, "A lot of us are born Jews; she *chose* to be Jewish." Rabbi Fine spoke at every event after Lillian's death. Her funeral, the end of saying daily Kaddish (memorial prayers said daily for a person who has died) and the day we unveiled her tombstone. I have nothing but respect and gratitude for his presence in our lives.

We held our wedding at the Jewish Community Center in Scranton on a beautiful snowy day that also happened to be Superbowl Sunday (the only date they had available). We were married by the rabbi who'd supervised Lillian's conversion. My maternal grandfather walked Lillian down the aisle because her father couldn't come under the canopy. Her sister Diane was the maid of honor, and my best man was Frank Labaty, a musician friend of mine who I'm still close to today; I consider him like a brother, and his parents in many ways are like my adoptive parents.

Several times, during the ceremony and reception, I looked around and found no men in the audience: they were all out trying to get the Superbowl score. It was Superbowl IX on January 12, 1975, and the Pittsburgh Steelers beat the Minnesota Vikings.

We went to Acapulco on our honeymoon, to a place called Las Brisas. We had a cabana with a private swimming

I COULDN'T DO THIS ALONE, I HAD HELP

pool, into which they'd throw flowers every morning. It was more than we could afford, but we figured we'd pay it off in time. (One of Lillian's uncles, who everyone thought was "connected," kept asking where we were going; If I told him, maybe we wouldn't have had to pay for anything, but I kept mum. The location of the honeymoon was a surprise for Lillian; I only told her, "Bring warm-weather clothes!"

My 40-year marriage to Lillian was the greatest blessing of my life. We were perfectly suited to each other. She was five years older than I, which I always said was for the best because otherwise, I'd never have been able to catch her. She was so bright and talented, as well as being deeply intuitive—street smart and excellent at reading people. She did not suffer fools. I was habitually trusting, sometimes naively so, but Lillian could immediately sense a person's energy and true intentions. We complemented each other in other ways as well; she was deeply visual, while I was 100% aural. She always made our home look beautiful, but when she asked my opinion about a potential choice—"What do you think of painting this wall yellow?"—I never had much to say beyond, "I'll let you know when I see it." On the other hand, she loved music but had no ear for it. She couldn't carry a tune; you wouldn't recognize "Happy Birthday" if she wasn't singing the words.

We never fought in 40 years. It sounds odd to say, but it's true. Of course, we had minor arguments, plenty of differences of opinion, but never a real fight. I never had a

I COULDN'T DO THIS ALONE, I HAD HELP

single day when I wished I wasn't married.

I even loved the quirks of her personality, such as her inability to wait to open a gift. Our first Christmas together, I bought her a red scarf; I caught her sitting by the tree when she thought no one was watching her, poking at the seams in the wrapping paper and trying to figure out what it was. When I called out her name, she jumped about five feet in the air. She'd do the same thing to chocolates too when she got a box of them; she'd stick her nail in the underside of each and figure out what she wanted, no surprises.

When we first got married, we lived in an apartment that I'd had before we got married. Her brother came over and helped me repaint it. Her dad used to come over and leave us food on the back porch because he didn't think we could afford to buy our own. He had ties to many local farmers from whom he'd buy produce, so he'd give us eggs, beef, chicken, vegetables—you name it. He'd do that once a week for what must have been years. He was a very sensitive guy but never let it show—that's why he wouldn't wait around, just drop it on the back porch and go.

Her father was a tough guy and had connections to some unsavory people. She was the oldest daughter, so she spent a lot of time with her dad on the road with the fruit truck. He'd leave her by the roadside stand to sell produce; he'd go do whatever he did and come back and get her. Lillian's mother was lovely and very eccentric. She had lots of funny habits—like when she was housecleaning, she'd cut the elastic out of

I COULDN'T DO THIS ALONE, I HAD HELP

Jockey shorts and use that to tie her hair back. She was very proper about etiquette and had a very aristocratic air about her; she was German and Irish but always called herself "Bavarian." Her cooking was unforgettable; she'd do things like stuff ziti with a syringe. She'd learned for her husband's sake how to make Lebanese food; I never forgot the time she made kibbeh, a Lebanese dish made from raw meat and bulgur wheat. This one time, when we went to her mother's house to have kibbeh, it was orange. When we said, "Why is this orange?" she said, "Don't tell your father-in-law, but I put carrots in, because they're good for him." It tasted awful! But we all ate it. It was funny to see her together with her husband. She had these aristocratic airs and cared about things like how to set a table, while her husband was straight out of the streets. There was constant friendly conflict between them. "Don't do that, Joe! I'm gonna do it! I can do it! I always did it at my mother's!" At the end of the day, however, my in-laws treated me like a son and always made me feel welcome in their presence.

Lillian's brother, Ralph, was about 12 years younger than her; in many ways, she was like his mom. We got along famously from the start and are still quite close today. He always made me feel like part of the family, and I think of him as my own brother. We love each other unconditionally, which is really the best you could ask for from any person.

Lillian's grandmother had come from Lebanon. I remember being nervous to meet her for the first time, but

I COULDN'T DO THIS ALONE, I HAD HELP

she just gave me a hug and a kiss and said, "We're all the same people, honey." Her husband had died very young, and she had put her two girls through college at a time when that wasn't really done. She used to say, "I suffered with no husband—I don't want the same for them." She made a living by crocheting pillowcases and other white goods and selling them. After Lillian and I were married, her grandmother and I developed a ritual where I'd bring her fish and chips from Long John Silver's every Wednesday and we ate lunch together.

Our son, Joseph, was born about 20 months after we got married. When I found out Lillian was pregnant, I went out and bought a house. I thought this would be a nice surprise, but Lillian was upset that I'd done it without her. I surprised her a lot throughout our marriage; sometimes she appreciated it more than others, but she always knew my heart was in a good place.

Lillian had a very difficult pregnancy, so much so that at one appointment, I had to watch the doctors debate whether they would try to save her or the baby. Lillian had developed diabetes during the pregnancy, and the fetus was developing more slowly than usual, so they were debating whether to take him out early and how soon it would be safe. After that appointment, in Scranton, we decided to get a second opinion at Hershey Medical Center. There, they were much more reassuring; they didn't think it was a life-or-death issue. They told us that the gestation period would

I COULDN'T DO THIS ALONE, I HAD HELP

just be much longer than normal. In the end, Joseph was born almost 11 months after he was conceived.

He was a big baby, almost 11 pounds. At the time, partners weren't allowed in the delivery room unless they'd taken a special course; I took it and felt like I was practically a doctor by the end, but then the baby was delivered by C-section, so I couldn't go. I remember going to see him in the nursery. Because the hospital dealt with a lot of complicated pregnancies, many of the babies were severely premature; I remember looking through the window and seeing row after row of tiny babies. Then the nurse caught my eye and pointed down—there was Joseph, over 10 pounds, with a full head of hair, practically picking his head up already. Lillian and Joseph bonded right from the start. They adored each other all the way up to her death.

Joseph was a brilliant child, smart from the beginning. But he was late to potty train and late to break from the bottle, so they wouldn't accept him at the local Hebrew preschool. He went to Montessori instead; he loved it there. The principle of Montessori is that they give you boundaries, and within those boundaries, you're free to explore. You can go to the book section and read any book you like or go to the blocks section and build. Joseph was always pushing boundaries from the start: "What if I want to read a book *and* build with blocks? What if I want to do both while tap-dancing? Can I do that in the blue section?" One of my favorite stories from Montessori was when the teacher pulled us aside one

I COULDN'T DO THIS ALONE, I HAD HELP

day and asked us, gently, if we could do something about Joseph's breath. He loved garlic from an early age, and it turned out he was grabbing a couple of cloves on his way out the door and chewing them on the way to school.

Joseph started playing piano very young; he studied with my teacher until she passed away. Later, he played glockenspiel in the marching band. Lillian and I enjoyed watching him grow up and become a person with his own interests, opinions, and skills.

Work Life

In college, I always said that the two things I *didn't* want to do were 1) selling things and 2) working with computers. And what did I end up doing in my first job? Selling computers.

The job was with Burroughs, a computer manufacturer (William Seward Burroughs was the inventor of the adding machine; that's how they got started). My first boss was a guy named Frank Shevets. This was during the very first stages of computers being available to small business enterprises— the last days of posting machines. Univac introduced to the public huge machines that they saw on television predicting the outcome of presidential elections—monstrous computers the size of a football field.

Everyone at Burroughs started by selling adding machines. Then you moved your way up— calculators,

I COULDN'T DO THIS ALONE, I HAD HELP

posting machines, and finally, computers. Our clients were mainly banks, as well as hotels and high-volume retailers. My territory consisted of banks, savings and loans, and insurance agents.

It was interesting being present for the early days of computers. I remember once bringing a portable computer in to show Joseph's elementary school class. It was the size of a suitcase; I had to lug it in on a hand truck. I taught the students a basic lesson on how to do binary mathematics, and they were fascinated by it.

IBM was our main competitor, and I learned a lot about sales from being up against them. I often had people tell me, "IBM is much more expensive than you, but nobody ever got fired for buying IBM. If I buy Burroughs and it doesn't work out, then they'll say, 'Why didn't you buy IBM?' But if I buy IBM, I can always say, 'I don't know what happened, I bought the biggest and the best!' and I won't be blamed for it." My response was "Why do you believe you won't be held accountable for the outcome regardless of the brand? If you buy Burroughs then you've bought me. I'm going to give you a list of every client I have and you can call them and ask what their experience has been with Burroughs and with me. Then tell me how you called IBM's references and let me know which PERSON you want to trust with this task." You may not win them all, but I won more than my share and I never left a client with less than I promised them. When I left Burroughs to go with United

I COULDN'T DO THIS ALONE, I HAD HELP

Gilsonite Labs, I spent 3 months finishing a program for a customer without compensation and without any obligation to do it. I gave my word and that made all the difference.

I brought the "never lie" attitude I'd gained in the military to my job as a salesman. I remember one time when I met with a woman who worked at a concrete company. She said she was likely going to buy a machine from NCR (National Cash Register, one of our competitors). I told her, "I have to tell you, in all honesty: What they're telling you they'll be able to do, they won't be able to do. We can't do it either, but I want you to know that they're overpromising." She said, "But they promised me . . ." I just shrugged and said, "I'm giving you the honest truth!" She ended up buying the NCR machine, and in about six months, she called me back and said, "They couldn't do it!" I said, "I tried to tell you that." Though I'd lost the sale, I gained a reputation as an honest salesman.

I learned however, that selling the machines sometimes involved a certain amount of showmanship and perhaps stretching the absolute truth a bit. Once, we had a demonstration for Bank of America—the first big account I ever had. This was still in the era of posting machines; we had a new model (the last posting machine model, it would turn out) that featured ledger cards with a readable stripe, like ATM cards. It all took place on a piece of paper but was the last step before computers with screens. NCR had recently come out with a posting machine that had a

I COULDN'T DO THIS ALONE, I HAD HELP

typewriter attached to it. We didn't have one like this, so we came up with a campaign making it seem unnecessary—*What's in a name? What do you need a name for? Numbers, that's what's important! You don't need a typewriter!* But meanwhile, we were developing our own version of the typewriter-attached machine. When ours came out, six months later, we of course changed our marketing strategy. So I had this presentation at Bank of America—we were trying to sell them the new posting machine for their tellers. NCR was our competition. We were still fine-tuning the machine; it would make one transaction and then lock up. We knew we could fix it, but the updated version wasn't ready in time for the presentation. So we brought in four machines and lined them up next to each other. We performed the transaction, flawlessly, on the first machine and then said, "Now, what are the chances the next guy who comes in will go to the same teller? It needs to work at every machine in the room!" So we'd go to the next machine, then the next and the next—thus avoiding using the same machine twice and running into snags. Then we walked the executives outside and continued our pitch, while our mechanics came in and scrambled to free up the machines.

Burroughs had an incentive commission, so each salesman had a monthly goal that they needed to try and achieve. You got 8% commission up to your goal, and once you hit your goal, you got 13% of everything you sold beyond that for the rest of the month. So when you hit 13%, you learned to close

I COULDN'T DO THIS ALONE, I HAD HELP

like nobody's business. My skills grew, and I got promoted to be a zone sales manager, with three salesmen working for me; we'd go out sometimes to make calls together, and I'd have my own territory in addition to that. Some of the guys I worked with are still my friends today.

When I became a zone sales manager, Burroughs told me my next job was to go to Detroit, where their home office was. But I didn't want to go to Detroit. They told me that if I didn't move, I'd stay a zone sales manager for the rest of my life—there was no other way to advance. That's when I decided I should find something else to do.

Eventually, I went to work for one of my clients, United Gilsonite Laboratories (UGL); they made car polyurethane coatings and Beverlee satin stain. I became their head of IT. For all intents and purposes, I was the CIO. I had people working for me by the time I was done, and in the seven or eight years I was there, they tripled their sales volume. UGL was a small family-owned business that became one of the largest distributors in the country, yet when I came in, they had a very antiquated system. Even though I'd sold them a computer, they used it for very little—just for keeping track of money. Once a month, everyone had to work the entire weekend to take inventory, so they'd instituted a 36-hour work week in order to get around paying overtime. So I computerized everything—wrote custom programming from scratch, in collaboration with Tom Stoddard (I did the program definitions, and he did the programming).

I COULDN'T DO THIS ALONE, I HAD HELP

This enabled us to reduce the amount of time needed for inventory to only 90 minutes. Needless to say, the employees were grateful to have their weekends back. And they still let them work just 36 hours per week!

Tom Stoddard is someone I stayed in touch with; he was at my son's bar mitzvah, and I still call him three or four times a year to see how he's doing. He's a 3rd- or 4th-generation dairy farmer—he studied optical physics at MIT and then decided to join the family business. I used to take Joseph up to Tom's farm to see the dairy cows; Tom had a son about Joseph's age. Tom would always tell them, "Don't run in the cow barn!" One day, we heard this awful scream. Joseph, against Tom's warning, had been running in the cow barn with Little Tom; Joseph had tripped and fallen into cow manure. He was completely covered, head to toe; all you could see was his eyes. Tom yelled, "Stop right there!" He got a hose and washed Joseph down—but even after he was washed off, the smell was so bad that we had to have the windows down the whole way home. That experience was so unforgettable that Joseph wrote about it as part of a college application essay (the prompt was "Tell us about an embarrassing thing that happened").

At UGL, I had the chance to influence company policy beyond the scope of my initial job description. As we automated operations and freed up people, we found more interesting work for them. Our customer service people had to learn to use computers, making me the logical person to

I COULDN'T DO THIS ALONE, I HAD HELP

take over the new customer service position. So I started to learn a lot about areas outside of sales and computers. After we integrated handheld terminals for our salespeople in the field—they'd used to have to go write an order by hand, but we introduced something called a Telzon terminal—I had to teach the salespeople how to use it, so I wound up running sales. Because I had sales experience myself, we'd collaborate on strategy: they would teach me about the product, and I'd share my ideas for the best way to sell something. Essentially, whenever they computerized anything, I got to do it.

Gerald Payne was the owner of the company. He told me once, "Just remember, Marshall: Every dollar I have in my pocket came from someone else's." I don't think I took that attitude to heart in that way—it struck me as ruthless so I reworked the axiom: "NEVER forget that your customers need to trust you before they share their money with you in order for your business to thrive. So treat them like the important asset they are." Being in the army had taught me how to take opinions I didn't necessarily agree with and yet make the most of them. Mr. Payne and I got along famously because, though I didn't necessarily use his methods, I achieved the ends he was looking for.

When I'd gone as far as I thought I could go at my current salary, I asked for a raise. The response I got was, "You're very good at what you do, but we're not willing to pay more than such-and-such an amount for IT expertise. You'll get cost of living increases, plus a little bit more, but we can't

I COULDN'T DO THIS ALONE, I HAD HELP

do much else." I wasn't upset at this response; they were a family-owned business, they didn't have infinite resources, and I appreciated their honesty. I just responded, "I have to tell you, then, that I'm going to look and see if I can find something else."

I started looking for another job, and Burroughs offered to take me back—they'd even let me skip the Detroit move and put me in New York. I went to New York for the interview and saw *A Chorus Line*, which was the big Broadway show at the time. Burroughs offered me the job—with about a 50% increase over what I was making. It seemed like a great opportunity, and I accepted. But when I went to New Jersey to try and find a house, I realized that the 50% salary increase would be more like 2% once you factored in cost of living. Plus, I'd have a 45-minute commute. I envisioned a future in which my family was just scraping by, surrounded by neighbors who were making much more. So I rethought the offer and told them I didn't want the job after all. I still remember the note I got from Bill Heverly, the guy who'd solicited me for the job: "The King has no balls." He thought I didn't have enough guts to take the leap of faith. I just responded, "Oui, oui." I'd made my decision.

I went back to UGL and asked if they'd found anyone else to take my place. They said they hadn't, and I asked if I could have my old job back. They agreed. This was possible because we'd all been honest, forthright, and amicable at the

I COULDN'T DO THIS ALONE, I HAD HELP

time of my departure; the owner (who was the son-in-law of the founder) said, "I'd have done the same thing if I were you. Don't be afraid to walk in here and tell us you've found something else if you really want to do it and you're sure. Just stay with us until you know for certain that you want to go." I really appreciated that, and I ended up working there another two years.

In 1984, I got a call from Sherri Patterson the sister of the guy who was the best man at my wedding. She was working for a company named Guard Insurance, and they needed someone "who spoke both English and Nerd." I came there first as a consultant to lay out a staffing and salary matrix for them; they were in the process of forming a separate I-T company out of what had been the private insurance operation. This was called Datavest. When I was done with the consulting work, they said, "How would you like to head up this organization?" I had designed it, so I thought it was pretty good; I took the job, and I was there for 32 years.

The founders of the company, Susan and Judd Shoval, became very important people in my life. Susan was born in Wilkes-Barre and had gone to Cornell; Judd was an Israeli and had a background in law. They had met when she had studied abroad in Israel. Susan was born with a silver spoon in her mouth, and a lot of people thought her parents had given them the money for the company. On the contrary, they did it all on their own They designed the company together; the first ideas were sketched out on a napkin over

I COULDN'T DO THIS ALONE, I HAD HELP

dinner (they still have the napkin). When I interviewed with them, Judd told me his vision for the company. He said, "I think this company is going to be like Travelers someday. If you want to be a part of it, you can invest your life in it." He was a great visionary, while Susan was the one who put flesh on the bones. Judd was the only guy I ever told, "You're a better salesman than me."

I was their 37th employee, and I started out as their I-T manager. We had a great relationship from the beginning. My strategy of total honesty paid off: Susan told me once that she said to Judd, of the guy who'd done the job before me, "You know, Mike used to promise me stuff and never deliver it when he said he would. I don't like Marshall's schedule, but when he says he's gonna have something done, it's really done!"

I used to tell Susan and Judd all the time, "You are great at customer service, but your organization is lousy at sales." For example, we were one of the only companies writing Workers' Comp premium in Pennsylvania. It tended to be a losing line of business, but we were profitable because we were very selective about the risks that we would write. Then, all of a sudden, the market softened up, and the industry raised the rates—suddenly, we had competition. Susan and Judd called me up and said, "You know, you've been telling us for years that sales are not what we do well."

I said, "That's right."

They said, "So, we need somebody in sales."

I COULDN'T DO THIS ALONE, I HAD HELP

I said, "Good—it's about time you hired somebody."

They said, "Do you want the job?"

That was the only time they ever shocked me.

I said, "Can I have my old job too?"

They said yes, I could do both jobs. So I took the job, we hired some additional people, and the salespeople became true salespeople. We had only been a Pennsylvania-based company, but we started to expand to Delaware, Maryland, the East Coast, and then nationwide.

We made sales, first and foremost, based on our experience and record. I'd tell people, "Why would you want to go with a company that wasn't profitable in Workman's Comp until they raised the rates? We've been profitable the whole time." I'd also tout our modest size and excellent customer service: "When was the last time the executive vice president of Hartford stood in front of you and said, 'I want your business?' I report directly to Judd and Susan; if you want their phone number, I'll give it to you, and they'll answer." Sometimes, Judd himself was on the sales call with me, and I got to say, "Look, this is the owner himself! If you want him, you can call him!" Another line I used a lot was, "We're not here for all of your business, only the best part."

We really were better at Workman's Comp than everybody else. We paid attention to the little things. For instance, if you know anything about medical billing, first visits to a doctor always cost more than subsequent visits. You wouldn't believe how many doctors billed two first visits. We

I COULDN'T DO THIS ALONE, I HAD HELP

computerized our system and enabled it to catch things like that. We had two doctors and two nurse practitioners help us design the program. This helped us catch other things; for example, if a doctor had picked the most expensive code for something that had multiple treatment codes, we'd call and ask why they'd chosen that one. We paid attention to all the pennies, which most insurance companies didn't do, and we profited. It was all built into the computer system; we called it "assistive adjudication."

Once a year, I used to spend a day working in customer service, just for fun. I'd go from one seat to the next, working for a few minutes at each. I had the customer service people right behind me, watching me try to do their jobs, and they would laugh because I was very nice to the customers, but I didn't know how to do anything. I'd apologize to the customer—"Sorry, Ma'am, I'm just in training." The customer service folks would enjoy the hell out of it. I'd say, "I do this to show you guys just how good you really are. I'm not cheating—if I could do it, I would. You guys handle a lot, you do it real well, and you're not always recognized for it, so thank you." I was always exhausted when I got done with my day there.

Judd and Susan were very generous with me and let me do far more than I would have normally been entitled to. I got to run a lot of things over time; I had a hand in almost every department in the company at one point or another, except for actuarial science and accounting and

I COULDN'T DO THIS ALONE, I HAD HELP

investments. This gave me broad experience that I could never have gotten anywhere else.

Guard was sold to an Israeli insurance company called Clal Insurance. They were seeking a way to acquire an insurer in the United States. That was the beginning of my relationship with Sy Foguel, our new CEO. Sy and I liked each other from the very beginning. He was a mentor to me and he actually changed my life in very tangible ways. He said early in our relationship that he would try to manage his manners but I should understand that he is an Israeli and if he interrupts me he's not necessarily being rude. Culturally, he said, Israelis don't want to waste your time when they are going to make the ultimate decision; if they don't agree with you, they just tell you to stop. It is difficult to see this as a benefit, but it is a cultural thing. Sy would sometimes get carried away when he was in a meeting with clients and I would sit next to him and literally kick him when he was going overboard. When I retired he said, "Who will kick me now?"

Sy was the most genuine man I met in business. In many ways he wore his heart on his sleeve. He was a brilliant actuary and an exceptional business strategist. He drove Guard into our future with Berkshire Hathaway. If not for Sy, this wouldn't have come to pass. When Berkshire Hathaway bought us, about 12 years ago, Sy and I stayed with Guard. He also knew that sales was not his strength, so he deferred to me many times; it takes an awfully big CEO

I COULDN'T DO THIS ALONE, I HAD HELP

to do that. We played off each other very well and I loved going to sales presentations with him. He taught me a lot.

Presenting to agents at a Berkshire Hathaway sales meeting.

Business Principles

Over the decades I worked for Burroughs, UGL, and Guard, I learned a lot about working with people. I could probably write a whole separate book just about those principles, but I'll outline a few of them here.

The first and most important principle was always "Treat everyone the way you want to be treated." That was the foundation of my whole management philosophy.

One way that this manifested was in the policies we instituted for employees and their families. I always said, "If you want your business to be a family business, hire

I COULDN'T DO THIS ALONE, I HAD HELP

the entire family." What I meant by that was that it was important to do things not only for the worker but for their spouse and children. This was baked into everything from company policy to small, personal gestures.

We had holiday parties and picnics to which partners and children were invited, for free. When they were present, I'd always make a point to thank them: "Your partners are great assets to the company—but *you* have to permit them to take the time to do their job well, and nobody does a job well without sacrifice. So thank you for allowing us to have the time and talents of your partner."

We wanted people to advance their education, if they chose to do that, because it made them better at whatever they did. So we paid for MBAs, free of charge. If an employee got their CPCU certification, we would give them a trip to the next CPCU conference. (Often there was a surge in certification when the next conference was in an exotic location, like Hawaii.) Every five years, the company would give employees money to take a vacation with their family: $2,500 at year five, $3,000 at year 10, $3,500 at year 15. The only rule was that you had to take a trip with the money. So people who had never dreamed of taking their family to Disney World got to do so, on the company, and they'd always come back with pictures for us. As a result, nobody ever left in year four, nine, or fourteen!

Care for the employee and their whole family manifested in smaller gestures as well. An employee once mentioned

I COULDN'T DO THIS ALONE, I HAD HELP

that his anniversary was coming up and asked me for a restaurant recommendation. I gave him the name of one, then called the restaurant and told them that I would pay for his bill. He was so grateful for that, and to this day, he still writes me notes to check in.

Another key principle of mine was to make sure that, from the very beginning, every employee had a direct line of sight to the value they provided to the organization. That's the only way you can ask them to contribute; if they don't understand their value, then it's harder for them to provide it. For example, I once asked the receptionist what her job was. She responded, "Well, I answer the phone . . ." I said, "No, your job is to make everybody that comes through that door or talks to you on the phone feel like they're a valued partner in this company. Your job is to make them feel at home. You are the Vice President of First Impressions." And she did just that; she always made people smile as soon as they walked in the door.

The next thing is to make sure that everyone knows they're going to be recognized for their work and that you're not going to take credit for it. Prove it to them early! I'd tell the managers to look for something a person did that was notable and send it to me in an email; I'd then forward it to the CEO, and he would write them a note recognizing their good work. For example, "We had guests in the building today; they commented on how clean it was and how it looks spectacular for an old building, so I want

I COULDN'T DO THIS ALONE, I HAD HELP

to thank the maintenance department for the great work they do." Everybody wants to get a letter from the CEO, so you start to get very healthy competition for that kind of recognition. Plus, it proves to people that you're not going take credit for their work. I always said, "I can bask in the reflected glory of your accomplishments, and I don't need to take credit for them."

I believe strongly in nurturing people's talents and promoting folks from within. I was involved in promoting a number of people over the years to Vice President who had started with me as employees. They were great workers, great accomplishers—so why not? We knew that they showed up, that they were responsible, and that they understood the company. Of course we made sure they were qualified but what they already proven was something you couldn't reliably get from someone outside the company. The first employee I ever hired is, in fact, still with the company. He was the only person I hired without a bachelor's degree. But he was so anxious to get the job and so obviously well-disciplined that I just couldn't avoid hiring him. He finished his Bachelor's on the company's credit, and he's now in charge of all our physical facilities.

I've interviewed a lot of people in my life, and one counterintuitive thing I've come to look for is a team performance background. Whether it's drama, music, or team sports, I know a couple of things about you if you've had such an experience: I know that you have the discipline

I COULDN'T DO THIS ALONE, I HAD HELP

to practice something on your own, that you can also work in a group, that you can follow directions. I know you're competitive, and I know that you know how to win *and* lose. This principle almost always resulted in really good hires; I even hired four people right out of the Wilkes Civic Band.

Once hired, it's important to make sure that people know what their career path is and what it will take to get there. Help them understand how to go about moving there. If they can see the future, they will work toward it.

If you treat people this way, you'll retain them—and if you promote them from within, you'll have experienced employees everywhere, which is always an asset. Novices kill you at two points: first, they don't know anything, and second, they often take the energy of your most talented people, who are required to monitor their work. Much better to hang on to an employee if they're good—then they become an incredible asset for the company. That's an indisputable axiom in my book.

I tried to give people increasing areas of responsibility. For example, the people who answered our phones never just read from a script, and you always got a live person when you called us—you were never sent to voicemail hell. As a result, the people who answered the phones had to know a good deal about company policy and operations, since they were actually answering questions themselves in real time. This made their job more interesting while also

I COULDN'T DO THIS ALONE, I HAD HELP

giving the people in each department more time to do high-priority work. So everybody benefited.

As a result of all of these policies, we had high levels of productivity—and when someone wasn't pulling their own weight, their department would usually take care of it. In a strong department, where people are working at capacity and using their talents and working as a team, you want to do your part. You can see everybody else tasking themselves and holding themselves to a high standard, and it becomes infectious.

When we were for sale (when Berkshire Hathaway ended up buying us), we had people from other insurance companies coming in who had approximately the same number of policies, the same premium volume, and yet *three times* the number of employees. And it wasn't that we pinched pennies and cut corners on anything—it was that we empowered employees to do more work and gave people an appropriate level of responsibility.

Another important principle is to grow people into your replacement as best you can. From the very beginning, have an eye on who might grow into your position so that if you get hit by a bus, someone will at least be able to put their finger in the dyke until they can hire somebody new. There are so many things you can't control, so you have to learn to control the things you can.

I always had a policy of intellectual honesty. I didn't want to just hear what people thought I wanted to hear; I wanted

I COULDN'T DO THIS ALONE, I HAD HELP

to hear what people really thought. I always listened to them with genuine openness, even if I didn't end up using their ideas. There were never repercussions for sharing your opinion—though there might be repercussions for not rowing with the team once a decision had been made. I always appreciated Warren Buffett's line about knowing the difference between a bad decision with a great outcome and a great decision with a bad outcome. If you really want to empower people to take chances on ideas, you have to be willing to say, "It was a great idea—it just didn't pan out." Then you have to be able to move on. Once they see you do this, people internalize it and become more willing to take risks.

I had a cousin who worked for us once say, "You know, people are really nice to your face." I just laughed and said, "Really?" I've never held the illusion that I could make everybody happy. You're going to make some decisions that people just don't care for—or perhaps they just don't care for you. But as long as their work ethic is appropriate, and their performance is good, there's no reason you have to earn their approval in everything you do—you can't please everyone anyway, so you just have to make the best call you can in each situation and take responsibility for it.

This means, also, owning up to it when you're wrong. If you're willing to say, "I'm very sorry, I made a mistake, I shouldn't have done that," you'll reap the rewards a thousand times over, because people will know that they can

I COULDN'T DO THIS ALONE, I HAD HELP

trust you and that you won't let your ego get in the way of a good decision.

Another short-but-sweet principle: If you surprise an employee with a bad evaluation, *you've* done a terrible job. If he doesn't know in advance what the issues are, how is he supposed to fix them?

It was really important to me to get to know everyone in the company, as best I could. I had an elevator speech, tailored to the length of the elevator ride and how long I knew each person. When I had 20 seconds with someone I'd never met before, I'd say, "Hi, I've never seen you before—what's your name, what's your department? I'm Marshall Kornblatt, I'm the EVP of operations here. You've got a great department—Sean, the manager of your department, is an excellent manager. Talk to him about anything you need, I'm sure he wants to see you succeed. If you ever need me for anything, I'm on the fifth floor, in the corner office—just come see me." If I already knew the person, I'd say, "Hey, Charlie, how you doing, how's the job going, you comfortable with everything? Enjoying yourself while you're here?" I had 15 seconds for people I knew well, 15 seconds for people I didn't know well, 15 seconds for people I didn't recognize, and 15 seconds for vendors. A little attention like that can go a long way; especially with new people, it can have a huge impact.

When people called me "Mr. Kornblatt," I'd say, "Please don't do that—call me Marshall." And I really meant it.

I COULDN'T DO THIS ALONE, I HAD HELP

People worked *with* me, not *for* me, and I really tried to put that attitude into everything I did.

What gave me the most satisfaction in every job I had was to see the success and accomplishment of those who worked with me and to watch them grow and advance.

They never forgot me, and I will never forget them.

Music

Meanwhile, all the way through college and throughout my entire working life, I was still a working musician.

Starting in college, I played six nights a week in the nearby Poconos, then advertised as the "Honeymoon Capital of the Country." I enjoyed it, and the money helped me through school—the GI Bill paid for my actual tuition, but the income from performing helped with living expenses.

When I'd just gotten out of college and taken the job with Burroughs, I had to go to a training program at Valley Forge, right outside of Philadelphia. I'd kept my Poconos gig to help through the transition, which meant playing six nights per week until 1 a.m. and then going to school in Valley Forge, starting at nine. I decided to hire someone who was in school with me to drive me to and from the gigs; he could sleep while we played, and I could sleep on the way back.

One night, though, he couldn't make it. I figured that I could handle one night of driving. After the show, around

I COULDN'T DO THIS ALONE, I HAD HELP

1 a.m., I started home. It was pouring rain. When I went to get off at my usual exit, the exit was closed, so I got back on the Turnpike. Stuck between exits, I had to figure out an alternate route; while I was doing so, I ran out of gas. I had no choice but to get out of the car and try to hitchhike. Picture it: It's pouring rain, and I'm standing by the side of the road with my thumb out, wearing a silver lamé jumpsuit. I looked like a drowned rat—and a strangely dressed one at that. Needless to say, nobody stopped.

Finally, an AAA truck with gas pulled up; someone must have told them at one of the exits that there was someone—or *something*—stopped by the side of the road. The guy took out his can of gas and started putting a few gallons in my tank.

Silver Lame' outfit; Art Ravioli- drums, Charlie Morris- sax, Pete DeMarzo- guitar, Me - keyboards, Chu Chu Clayborn - vocals

Just then, I heard on his CB radio, amidst the crackle of static, the word "Kornblatt." I knew immediately what had happened: Lillian had phoned the police because I hadn't called her as usual when I got home from the gig. "That's me!" I cried. "They're looking for me! Please call and let them know I'm OK." He did. Finally, within a few minutes, I was back on the road.

I COULDN'T DO THIS ALONE, I HAD HELP

Lillian had to tolerate a lot because I wasn't home much. But she was grateful for what the income did for our household. Still, there were limits. The day before our wedding, the Glenn Miller band called and asked if I wanted to go on the road with them. Lillian took the call and said no, telling them I was getting married the next day. But they wouldn't take her no for an answer; they called back until they reached me directly. I told them that I agreed with Lillian's decision and couldn't go on tour. They said, "If you want to get married first, you can meet us in Chicago on Monday!" I thought it was more important to go on my honeymoon.

I had a lot of musician friends in the Scranton/Wilkes-Barre area; some played professionally or toured, while others just played locally. I had a good friend who played Radio City Music Hall. Another friend—the drummer in my first band, Donald Bick—became very successful, playing for Deutsche Grammophon and for the National Symphony. (My sister once went to a National Symphony concert with her husband and, squinting down from the nosebleed seats, said, "I think I know the timpanist!" "No way," said her husband. But sure enough, there his name was in the program!)

It was a very tight circle of people, and when someone advanced, they'd often reach out and offer me an opportunity. Along the way, I got to play for people like Willie Nelson, Natalie Cole, George Burns, and Steve Allen.

I COULDN'T DO THIS ALONE, I HAD HELP

When our performing arts center brought in someone that didn't have a pianist who came with them, I was first call. We did the Coasters, the Temptations, The Drifters, Chuck Berry and a lot of other doo-wop singles and groups. That was a great time; I met a lot of the musicians the touring artist would bring with them, and then they'd call me if they were playing nearby.

Chuck Berry, one of Rock's founding fathers never held a rehearsal saying "Everybody knows my stuff" and we did especially Johnny Be Good. He demanded payment in cash before he went on stage. He was serious about it because he had been cheated so many times in the early 50's and 60's.

I once got to play for Bob Hope. (This was the later years; he was already using 3x5 cards to remember his jokes.) His wife, Dolores, who used to be a Ziegfeld girl, had this little Pomeranian under her arm the whole time. At one point, the dog got away from her and decided to hump the lead violinist's leg. He kept trying to kick the dog off, and she said, "Why are you doing that? He likes you!"

Another time, I played for Steve Allen, who was the original host of *The Tonight Show*—before Jack Parr, before Johnny Carson. Steve Allen was a great musician himself. He came over to me

That's me playing behind Steve Allen the original host of the Tonight Show.

I COULDN'T DO THIS ALONE, I HAD HELP

before the show and said, "I'm just going to ad lib with the audience—whatever I talk about, play a song that has something to do with it. So if I say 'China,' play 'Slow Boat to China' or something like that." The show started, and I did exactly what he said. I know a lot of tunes, so it wasn't too much of a challenge. When we were finished, he said, "That is as well as anybody has ever played for me." That was a really big compliment.

I played with a circus, which was a lot of fun. I still remember meeting all of the performers—actors, trapeze artists, clowns, and all—and watching the Native American guys they'd hired to set up the rigging, who'd walk along the girders with no safety net at all. I also remember the breakfast they'd give us: Pancakes with eggs on top. They traveled with their own chickens, so eggs were plentiful.

A performance with Acordia Chorale featuring Catherine Carter on vocals

Playing the nationally televised Easter Seal Telethon with Debby Dunleavy.

The Skytop Lodge Big Band in the Pocono Mountains. A great band with wonderful musicians I'm in the back right.

Phil Simon - bass, Tony Kurdilla - sax, Tom Frew - drums, Me - piano, Erin Malloy - vocals

Several Photos from an engagement in Scranton Pennsylvania.

I COULDN'T DO THIS ALONE, I HAD HELP

It was sometimes a challenge balancing work, music, and family. At one point, I held three jobs: I had a day job with Burroughs, was playing six nights a week, and was doing programming when I could fit it in after work. I kept up this schedule because I loved playing and also wanted my family to have the comforts that it had taken my own parents years to afford.

Mostly, though, I'm so grateful that I got into music when I did and found the kind of community I needed. That was a time when there were so many great jam sessions, where you could learn a ton from other musicians. Today, the opportunities aren't nearly as prevalent. I feel like I made it just in time for the last great era of jazz.

5

RETIREMENT

L illian and I had discussed my retirement a long time ago and agreed on a plan: I would work half time for two years and then retire completely. But about a year and a half into that plan, she passed away.

Lillian left the house that day to go get her hair done. About 30 minutes later, the hairdresser called and said, "I think she must have forgotten her appointment." But I knew she hadn't—something must be wrong. I called Joseph and told him to keep calling Lillian's cell phone, while I drove the route she'd likely taken. But only about 30 seconds after I'd left the house, he called me and said, "Dad, pull over. There's been an accident. She's gone."

She had apparently had some major medical incident while driving—a heart attack or aneurysm. There were no signs of struggle—the car had just gone off the road. Thankfully, no one else was hurt. The ambulance only took about 90 seconds to arrive because the EMT dispatch was just down the road, but when they arrived, she was

I COULDN'T DO THIS ALONE, I HAD HELP

not revivable. My daughter-in-law, Georgia, worked at the hospital where they'd taken her, and when they heard the name "Kornblatt," they asked if this was her relative. That's how my son had come to know so quickly.

The strange thing is that Lillian had always told me she'd die at 72. It was just something she felt certain about; I have no idea why. I'd always dismissed it as just a strange idea, but she was exactly 72 when she died.

The loss of her was devastating, of course, but as the person left behind, I found some saving grace in the fact that her death was likely quick and painless.

When we were planning her funeral, I remember speaking to the funeral home director and commenting that the 100 seats they had wouldn't be nearly enough. "Don't worry," he reassured me. "We've been doing this a long time—if we need to drag in extra chairs, we will." In the end, almost three hundred people showed up: Lillian's friends, my musician friends, my business contacts, people from all over the community. It was a testament to what a great lady she was: funny, generous, artistic, and sensitive. She was loved by so many people. The two rabbis that we were close to spoke, as well as Joseph. That day, it was so cold that everything was frozen when we took her to the cemetery. I stood there, so numb that I didn't even notice how cold I was. My sister, standing there next to me, noticed and wrapped her scarf around my ears, but it was too late, and I got frostbite. To this day, when it's really cold, I get a

I COULDN'T DO THIS ALONE, I HAD HELP

tingle around the tops of my ears, and it makes me feel like Lillian's watching me.

Though it's been a big adjustment to live without her, and I miss her every day, I mostly feel lucky that we had the wonderful 40-plus-year marriage that we had. It's a rare thing, and I never took it for granted.

After she passed away, I decided that since I didn't have a reason to retire any longer, I would stay at work. So I stayed another two and a half years. It was great to have someplace to focus my attention and energy. I finally retired at the end of January 2019.

My senior managers my retirement party. In center - me - to my left Carl Witkowski COO to my right (male) CEO Sy Foguel

Another picture from another room of employees at my retirement - I guess they all wanted to see me leave!

Liberace's mirrored piano he played at Radio City Music Hall.

Me playing Liberace's mirrored piano he played at Radio City Music Hall.
I signed the book with Elton John and Billy Joel.
There wasn't enough room to include this story. Ask me about it and I will tell you personally.

No trip to Japan is complete without the obligatory Mt. Fuji picture. Here SHE is!

A Shrine in Kyoto

A scene from the Buddhist monastery meeting room in Japan

...and here is the Monk and the monkey (that's me)

Our tour group for Japan

Sheva and me on our way to Meet Matisse

I COULDN'T DO THIS ALONE, I HAD HELP

About 11 years ago, Lillian noticed that I'd developed a habit of tapping my foot. "You should see a doctor," she said. When I went, they did a brain scan and told me it was too early to tell if I had Parkinson's or not and to come back in a year. But when we returned the following year, that doctor had left, and she was the only motion disorder specialist they had.

I called my sister, who was working at the University of Virginia at the time, and asked if she could recommend a doctor; she had a friend who was the head of motion disorders there. Her friend referred me to a good friend of his, Howard Hertig at the University of Pennsylvania. When I called Dr. Hertig's office, I was told that he wasn't seeing new patients, but my sister's friend called and got me in. When I saw the doctor, he said within five minutes of meeting me, "There is no doubt in my mind that you have Parkinson's."

I said, "Fine, OK. What do I do about it?"

He said, "You seem to be taking this very well."

I answered, "I was afraid you were gonna tell me I had ALS. In the grand scheme of terrible things, this is only about half as bad as I'd feared."

He said, "That's a great attitude."

But that's how I've always been: eternally optimistic, sometimes even to my own disadvantage. My attitude, when I face a challenge, has always been, *"Out of all the many people who've faced this challenge in the history of the world and succeeded,*

I COULDN'T DO THIS ALONE, I HAD HELP

I have to be smarter, or more determined than at least one of them. I'll figure it out."

Over time, since then, I've become something of a Parkinson's whisperer. As more people I knew hit their 70s, more of them got diagnosed with it. Because I was always open with people about my diagnosis, people began calling me when their relative or friend had been diagnosed and asking if I'd speak to them. I'm always happy to speak honestly about my experience and to give them some reassurance if I can. The thing I always tell people first is, "Parkinson's will not kill you." Something related might, it's true, but not the Parkinson's itself. It doesn't have to be a death sentence. My experience isn't the same as everyone's, but here I am, 11 years post-diagnosis, still doing all the activities of daily living—still even playing piano. Others may not be as fortunate, it's something they can't control Parkinson's is often cruel and punishing but keeping positive and doing as much as you are able is a good plan to follow. Asking for help when you need it is critical - it isn't a sign of weakness its a sign of maturity.

I have been very fortunate in my life; they say that "luck is opportunity meeting preparation," and I can take credit for the preparation but not for the luck. One of the ways in which I'm fortunate is that I've become financially comfortable enough to be in a position to help others. I've supported synagogues and summer camps and paid for scholarships for people who can't afford school or camp.

I COULDN'T DO THIS ALONE, I HAD HELP

I've also offered piano lessons free of charge to students who couldn't afford the fees.

I've made a point of looking out for musicians, since music can be a hard way to make a living. I regularly give to an organization called Jazz Bridge that helps struggling musicians. After COVID-19 shut down many musicians' performance schedules, I sent checks to several musicians I knew. I included a note that said something like, "You have stellar enough credentials that you could be a narcissistic jerk, but you're not. They say nice guys finish last, but hopefully not today. I know things are tough for musicians, and I want to offer this help, with nothing expected in return. I know what's probably going through your mind right now: *I didn't think we were that close!* To that, I'll just say that it's a privilege for me to hear you play and sometimes work with you, and I hope that this helps you out."

I've sometimes had people say, "You give away a lot of money!" and to that, I always say, "The person who gives you a dollar and goes without dinner because of it is the person who's sacrificed. This is not a sacrifice for me—it's a pleasure. I'm truly grateful and glad that I was able to help." I really mean this: it's true what they say, that the pleasure of receiving is nothing compared to the pleasure of giving.

I've always seen my money as something entrusted to me by a higher power; as such, I have an obligation to give back. I'm the caretaker of what I've earned, more than the owner; it only makes sense to give back to the community and to people who haven't had the advantages I have had. I can't take much credit for it, other than credit for the wisdom of trying to return some of the favors I've been granted.

In addition to financial giving, I've made an effort to give my time, especially since retirement. For example, I've served as president of the Jewish Home of Northeastern Pennsylvania. My own family has had need of the facility in the past, so I've been happy to be able to serve the organization.

In addition to volunteering, I've enjoyed the freedom of my retirement to connect with the many important people in my life. Joseph has a lovely wife named Georgia and two wonderful children. Both kids are embarking on careers: My granddaughter, Chava graduated June 2022 from George Washington University with a degree in public health and an interest in advocating for underserved communities, while my grandson, Shlomo, is studying avionics and has his FAA certificate for flying drones. He intends to become a commercial pilot. They have both taken a career track that involves some form of responsibility for others.

I COULDN'T DO THIS ALONE, I HAD HELP

My sister, Elayne, and I remain very close as adults, and I just adore her. She has a Ph.D. in Public Health and taught at the University of Virginia for many years while also consulting with organizations all over the world about how to handle needles so as to minimize the spread of AIDS and other blood borne pathogens. She has also become an expert in how to handle bodies properly for Jewish ritual burials in the time of COVID. Elayne is a living lesson in how to be gracious and not flaunt an intellect that is often well beyond your audience. I respect and admire her more than anyone else I can think of.

I make a point of staying in touch with the many wonderful people I've met over the years—from childhood friends, to buddies from the service, to fellow musicians, to colleagues from my work at Burroughs, UGL, and Guard. I often reach out to friends and past colleagues just to hear how they're doing.

I've been lucky in so many ways in my life, but the community I've built and the connections I've made are the real wealth. I feel privileged to have become a part of so many people's stories. My hope, in sharing my own story here, is that whoever reads this might find meaning or value in the experiences and lessons I've imparted.

In reading this book, I hope you will understand that I wasn't as smart as I may have appeared. I was lucky when fate made decisions like putting me in sales and computers or having my best friend's sister think of me when a job

I COULDN'T DO THIS ALONE, I HAD HELP

opened up at Guard.

So what can I take credit for? Surrounding myself with great friends who think as much of me as I do of them, taking a genuine interest in the people around me, and constantly improving myself by accepting challenges, not being bound by "that's the way we've always done it." If I could offer one piece of advice to my reader, it would be, treat everyone with kindness and respect. Not only do they deserve it, but it will pay dividends in more ways than you can imagine for the rest of your life.

Me and the next generation Lillian thanks to Jen and Dave!

Story Terrace

Made in the USA
Columbia, SC
06 August 2024